BECOME A WALKING WEAPON!

A Cheater's Guide to
Simple Skills, Practical Tactics and Other
"Dirty Little Secrets" of Self-Defense
You Can Learn, Use and Apply TODAY

by
Robert Bartkowski

Copyright © 820Express Enterprises
All rights reserved. No part of this book may be reproduced, scanned,
or distributed in any printed or electronic form without permission.
Printed in the United States of America
ISBN: 978-1-7932-2500-9

Contents

Contents 1
Disclaimer 2
Acknowledgements 3
Author's Note 5
Foreword 6
Preface 8
A Message to All Martial Artists 12
Chapter 1: Mental Training 15
Chapter 2 Preliminary Considerations 25
Chapter 3: Upper Body Techniques 60
Chapter 4: Lower Body Techniques 130
Chapter 5: Extreme Situations & Weapons Training 186
Chapter 6: Training Progression & Recommended
        Equipment. 191
Chapter 7: Recommended Reading & "Brain Training" ... 197
Final Notes & Parting Thoughts 206
Bonus Section: *Fighting Chance Fitness* Home Workout ... 207
Appendix A: 820Express Ving Tsun Martial Science Club ... 213
Appendix B: Wong Shun Leung Wing Chun Gung Fu 217
Appendix C: Philip Ng 220
Appendix D: Joseph Goytia 222
About the Author 223
Testimonials 224
Some Things to Keep In Mind 231
Dedication 234

Disclaimer

The adoption and implementation of the material offered in this book is at the reader's discretion and sole responsibility. The Author and Publisher of this book are not responsible in any manner whatsoever for any injury that may occur directly or indirectly from the use of this book.

Since the physical activities described herein may be too strenuous in nature for some readers to engage in safely, always consult a physician prior to training. The specific self-defense practices illustrated in this book may not be justified in every situation or under applicable federal, state or local law.

Neither the Author nor the Publisher makes any warranty or representation regarding the legality or appropriateness of any technique listed in this book.

Use this material at your own risk!

Acknowledgements

First and foremost to the Ng Family Chinese Martial Arts Association of Chicago, in particular Master Sam Ng, Sifu Philip Ng and my "Chinatown crew" of training brothers and sisters-thank you for allowing me to be part of a *kungfu* family in the purest sense of the word and for putting me on the path to true Ving Tsun, a lifelong study for me. I really do thank God every day that I stumbled upon your school that cold, dreary & blustery day back in 2002. A special thank you to my Sifu and close friend Philip Ng who, by following his dream of becoming an action film star in Hong Kong, has provided me with the inspiration and example to go after doing something I love and thus begin the process of making my passion my career.

To Sifu Joseph Goytia of Intense Defense Systems, thank you for exposing me to a real, battle-tested close-quarter combat system as well as exposing me to multi-faceted training methodologies, and for stressing the importance of both physical and mindset conditioning.

To Sifu Danny Cichocki (my "attacker" in the photo sequences) and the crew at Lee's Academy of Martial Arts, thank you for allowing me to continue my growth as a martial artist, a fighter and a person by allowing me to instruct (and thereby continue to learn) at your facility. I am more than honored to be a part of your family and know that our best years are still ahead of us.

To all of my other instructors of the past, in particular Master Chuck Williams of the Bei Shaolin Institute, Sifu Eric Balestri of the Chi Tai Lung Gung Fu Institute, Head Instructor Steven Wunder and the ATA "Survivors Academy" crew, Mr. Tim Rochford of Empower Training Systems, former Mexico City Golden Gloves champion Mr. Juan Salazar, legendary fight trainer and owner of the rough & gritty Chicago Boxing Club Mr. Sam Colonna, Laotian full-contact kickboxer Mr. Kaneda Matthaysack, 4th degree black belt former national judo champion Mr. John Kowal and classmate and fellow instructor Brian "The Kid from Crestwood" Reif, I say to all of you: I met you at various points throughout my martial arts journey, none of which were by accident. You have all left an indelible mark on me.

To my close friend Lariza Diaz, owner of Sweeping Dimensions Cleaning Service of Chicago, a heartfelt thank you for allowing me the opportunity to host self-defense workshops at your facility and thus providing me with many of the real-time action photo sequences used in this book, proving both the effectiveness of the techniques and concepts I teach as well as the ease of transmission of information for individuals regardless of age, strength or ability level.

To all those training partners-I dislike using the term "students" except when absolutely necessary for formalities' sake-I have the absolute privilege of instructing, you make me better myself each and every day. To say thank you for that is an understatement. You do a great job of keeping me on my toes and keeping my ego in check by smacking me around and forcing me to "walk the talk," and for that I am more and more grateful as time goes on.

To my family, thank you for shaping me into who I am today. I love all of you so very much. Thank you.

To my wife-the one person who knows how big a pain in the ass I can be more than anyone and yet still has not killed me in my sleep-thank you for being you. You make me want to be better at everything I do, and I can only hope to inspire you as much as you do me.

Thank You, God, for allowing me to share this point in time with all of the wonderful people listed above.

Author's Note

This informational product is trademarked under the seal of the
United States Copyright Office
Registration No. TXu1-278-382

No portion of this product may be reproduced without the expressed written consent of Robert Bartkowski.

Simply put: use this material, learn from it and make yourself and those around you better people. Nothing in this book is a new technique, I haven't "invented" anything, so you're free to use the information contained in this book however you see fit to enhance the lives of those around you. Just don't try and pass this particular work off as your own-it's illegal, immoral and most importantly, karma is a powerful thing. Just be honest and give credit where it is due-that's what I have done with material I've found to be valuable, and that's all I'm asking for.

I hope you find this product useful.

Foreword:
Who Am I and Why Should You Listen To Me?

Before I get into who I am, let's get straight with who I'm not.

I am *not* a 15th degree red, black and gold belt "Master" or "Guru" or anything else like that, by any stretch. I am *not* a former Green Beret, Army Ranger or Navy SEAL commando throat-cutting jungle fighter. I am *not* an extreme cage-fighting title belt holding world champion.

Now you may be asking yourself, "why is he telling me all of this? Isn't he afraid I am going to instantly toss his book on the scrap heap once he lets me know this?" Nope. Not at all. Why? Think about it for a second: I don't know about you, but I learn best not from someone whose resume is the most stacked or loaded with ranks, titles and trophies but from someone who can relate to me and who can transmit information to me in a manner in which I can easily grasp what is being taught, retain it and apply it when a situation calls for it.

So many self-defense programs out there rely on the resume of the instructor as credence for the subject matter when in reality *the only thing that matters is whether or not the person being taught can glean the essence of what is being taught.* If not, I don't care if the instructor has more medals than General Patton and a wall full of certificates, trophies and shiny championship belts, you won't learn what you need to learn and your time will not have been most constructively used. The best instructors have the right mix of ability and relatability, and the only merit one has as an Instructor is whether or not one can take people to a higher level of proficiency through his/her teachings.

I have no problem whatsoever in stating that I am simply a dedicated practitioner of the arts since 1994 (whose background includes traditional martial arts, combat sports and reality-based / military close quarter combatives) who has learned a thing or two that I feel might benefit the general public. One thing I have noticed through my years of study is the gap that typically exists between what works in the class, or the sparring competition, and what works in reality. Trying to "close that gap" is what this book and system I have developed is all about.

It is my wish that anyone reading this never needs to use what they are about to learn, however, to truly be at peace one **must** possess the ability to be vicious and ruthless. How can you have one side of the coin but not the other? These techniques will inflict damage to an attacker, and they can be applied regardless of how strong or weak, big or small, short or tall you are. I sincerely feel these principles and techniques can benefit decent people and the public at large, given today's crazy world in which we live, which is why I went through all the trouble to put my thoughts down on paper. If just one person reading this is able to utilize just one concept, idea or (God forbid) a technique from this book should the need ever arise, I would gladly write it a hundred times over.

Robert Bartkowski

Preface

First things first, THANK YOU for your interest in honest, realistic personal protection and self-defense! Before we dive right in to the "meat and potatoes" of what this book is all about, let's first define exactly what the *Walking Weapon Self Protection Skills System* is all about.

This System was developed by "yours truly," dedicated self-defense professional Robert Bartkowski with one goal in mind: to give the general public the simple, practical and effective tools necessary to survive a self-defense encounter.

All of the techniques are based on gross motor skills, so there are no fancy or complicated patterns to memorize.

All of the techniques are aimed at an opponent's vital targets: eyes, throat and groin.

All of the techniques are based on the concepts of simplicity, effectiveness and practicality.

All three factors involved in any encounter-the psychological, the emotional and the physical- are addressed equally.

Most importantly, the *Walking Weapon Self Protection Skills System* is based on a "proactive" rather than a "reactive" mindset, meaning that although we use the term "self-defense" generically, this is not a "self-defense" course- it is a self-PROTECTION course. You CAN protect yourself!

This system is made up of techniques, principles and strategies that enable people of all ages, fitness levels and body types to effectively remove themselves from physical confrontations. The reason for their effectiveness lies in their efficiency and in the scenario training that is utilized in our classes and live workshops.

This is not another "technique" based system, nor is it just a re-hash of traditional martial arts techniques that require years of dedicated practice in order to be used effectively. Rather, it is a system designed of nothing but *simple*, *practical* and *effective* techniques pulled from both traditional martial arts as well as modern military close quarter combat training combined with verbal diffusion patterns, attitude and mindset conditioning, situational awareness training and scenario drills designed to elicit the rush of emotions and chemicals encountered in a real life encounter.

I wish to impart to all those who read this importance placed on the ability to recognize and avoid potentially hostile situations as well as the ability to diffuse situations verbally and with body language. Only as a last resort do we resort to the ability to physically remove oneself from a dangerous situation in the most simple, effective and practical way by targeting the vital areas of an attacker in an unrelenting yet precise manner. Above all, I wish to give all those who read this or train with us the greatest tool one can have: Confidence. If someone never has to use this system, I consider that a victory. However, if someone must utilize what I teach and gets home to his/her family that night, I cannot ask for anything better.

What's In a Name?

The reason behind the name of this system, **Walking Weapon**, is simply this:

No one is helpless. NO ONE.
Be it a young person, teenager, middle aged office executive, soccer mom, or senior citizen - ALL are capable of inflicting damage on any attacker with the tools (hands, feet, elbows, knees and so on) that God gave them. My point is that every person on Earth is just as equally capable of being an attacker's worst nightmare as they are of becoming his next victim.

What separates the "victim" from the "survivor" can be boiled down to one thing:

PROPER TRAINING, BOTH PHYSICAL AND MENTAL.

It seems that as people become more and more "civilized," they lose sight of the fact that in an emergency, it's just YOU and what YOU CAN DO to save yourself and those close to you. This reality requires a certain "warrior spirit" and personal belief that- while you wish to live your life, go about your day and tend to your own business- if the situation should ever arise, you would know- not hope, not guess, but KNOW-that you *are* the baddest thing in the land and God help anything or anyone that gets in your way...and that's that.

Second, it is my belief that the martial arts' spiritual benefits such as peace of mind, clarity of purpose and harmony with others **can only be attained when one trains honestly and openly, confronting one's fears in training so they do not hinder them in real life.** This will lead to one keeping a level head, and remaining calm and collected even in the face of an emergency. The *Walking Weapon Self Protection Skills System* imparts to its students that while surviving any encounter is never only about learning physical techniques, as knowledge in all of the aforementioned areas is the only way to honestly approach proper self defense training, the techniques learned must be simple, practical and effective in order to be successful. This philosophy of personal protection can best be summed up in our motto, **"the LESS you have to remember, the MORE you have to work with."**

Contrary to popular belief, no special training is needed for this. How? Simply visualize, *I mean really visualize,* a 6'5" 275lb. behemoth who just guzzled a fifth of Wild Turkey wanting to pulverize you. Picture in your mind's eye someone who wants to rape and strangle your loved ones. Put yourself in the position of the heroes of United Flight 93, because in reality that could just as easily be you or me tomorrow. Practice with INTENT, PRECISION and COLD-BLOODED RUTHLESSNES and train with the mentality that it's not just your life; it's your family's lives as well.

Sound brutal? Sound violent? No shit it does-and whether we like it or accept it or not, that's just the way it is. As I begin each of my workshops and seminars I lay it out there just like that and remind those in attendance that if they cannot or refuse to grasp that concept then they had best, in the words of Bruce Lee, "learn to endure or hire a bodyguard and lead a less aggressive life."

A MESSAGE TO ALL MARTIAL ARTISTS...

The Author (center) with Senior Instructor Kenneth Lee (left) and Sifu/Head Instructor and current Hong Kong action film star Philip Ng (right) at the Ng Family Chinese Martial Arts Association headquarters in Chicago's Chinatown.

A note to all martial artists reading this: I am, have always been and will always be a traditional martial artist. The Ving Tsun (Wing Chun) system as taught to me by the Ng Family Chinese Martial Arts Association is, and will always be, my root and base. The *Walking Weapon Self Protection Skills System* is one that, because it is guided by the same concepts and theories (simplicity, efficiency and directness) as the Ving Tsun system, can be seamlessly integrated with any traditional martial art system or style, as these techniques are universal. What this system does, in effect, is isolate the *self preservation* aspect of the arts so that one does not need to study for years in order to gain this benefit.

I will always be indebted to traditional martial arts and I will always recommend their study to anyone, as the benefits are endless. In fact, it is my wish that by studying the material presented in this book, one not only receives the essence of self-defense training distilled in its most potent form thereby enabling one to protect him/herself should the need arise, but also the desire to explore any of the myriad of traditional forms of martial art.

In my opinion, martial arts are (or should be) in essence **fighting** arts. The benefits so often attributed to their study-increased self-confidence, concentration, awareness, fitness, good grades in school and so on-can most quickly be gained by returning to the essence of what the martial arts were created for: self-preservation and combat. It is up to all instructors of any system of martial art to return to the essence of what each of these beloved systems was created for. Too often martial arts have degenerated into little more than either a series of physical movements or a purely academic study in history, culture, etc. Both are totally fine, and both can coexist as long as one does not lose sight of the true purpose behind each of the arts we enjoy, practice and teach. True confidence comes from knowing you can take care of yourself in a physical encounter against someone who wants to hurt, rape, maim or kill you-period. Once that scenario is embedded in your mind, everything else one may face in the course of a day seems a bit more toned down in comparison.

I ask all instructors and martial art practitioners reading this to examine their art a bit more closely. Each of the techniques in this book can be found in your *katas* or forms-I haven't created a new way of moving. There are only so many ways to kick, punch, twist, choke, strike, chop and so on. It is up to you to and me as torch-bearers of our respective lineages and systems to "keep it real" so that as instructors we do not commit the gravest of sins against our students: infusing them with a false sense of confidence-one based solely on belts, certificates and, as Bruce Lee once stated, "nothing but blind devotion to the systematic uselessness of practicing routines or stunts that lead nowhere." Rory Miller, a former soldier, noted author, corrections officer and self-defense /personal protection authority figure stated once that "listening to average martial artists talk about real world violence is like listening to 10-year olds talk about sex." Hearing that may be a bitter pill to swallow for many folks out there, but it is one that needs to be swallowed if we all are to do right by our students.

Please read the following pages in this spirit.

"Self defense is a short list of techniques that may get you out alive when you're already screwed."
-Rory Miller

CHAPTER 1
MENTAL TRAINING
Proper Attitude, Mindset And Mentality

Mental Training

This section on proper mindset, attitude and mentality was originally going to be included in the next chapter but I felt after much thought that it deserves its own section-after all, mental training is hands down the most overlooked yet most important aspect of self-defense training. Don't believe me? No problem. Go to any shopping mall martial arts school that offers a "self-defense" class and I'll bet my left pinkie finger that within ten minutes you will be working on defenses against a wrist grab or a choke or whatever. At the end of the class you will have a mental suitcase full of techniques for damn near every possible scenario you can think of-and most likely next to nothing regarding mental training. It's a shame that so many folks out there try to address self-defense and personal protection from an "outside-in" approach (i.e., learning techniques to deal with any of the numerous situations one may find oneself in) when the fact of the matter is that true self-defense begins not with the hands or the feet but what is between your ears. Proper mental training leads increased self-confidence, a strong, assertive body language, a calm and collected demeanor and increased awareness to your surroundings. This can be akin to the old samurai warrior that walks through the battlefield without a scratch because he truly believes in his heart he won't be touched. I believe that such complete devotion to a belief leads the Universe to open up and part ways for you.

In a more pragmatic and immediately applicable sense, if I was a mugger, rapist or thug would I go after someone who appears confident, alert and attentive? No. I am a coward, which is why I am a mugger, rapist or a thug. I want to go after the girl jogging with her iPod on, oblivious to her surroundings. I want to assault the man walking down the street; shoulders slumped, feet shuffling, head down. I want to zero in on the person giving off signs of trepidation, fear or insecurity. Just as the cheetah goes after the weakest, slowest or smallest impala or wildebeest, I do not pick the hard target. I choose to hone in on whoever looks like the easiest mark for me. And I can tell right away based on a potential victim's body language, as that provides a window into his or her attitude and mentality.

Lessons from The "Deadliest Man Alive"

No figure in the history of martial arts in America has been surrounded by as much controversy as John Keehan, alias "Count Dante," the self-proclaimed "Deadliest Man Alive."

A once-respected *sensei* (karate instructor) and the one person most responsible for entrenching the martial arts in Chicago and the Midwest during the early to mid-1960's, after parting ways with his instructor he began promoting himself as the "Crown Prince of Death" and offered his booklet, *World's Deadliest Fighting Secrets*, for sale in the back of comic books. An absolute attention hound and fierce self-promoter, he would walk his pet lion down Michigan Ave. and Lake Shore Drive in a top hat and a cape, claimed to have been descended from Spanish nobility (apparently choosing to ignore the obvious fact that he was a red-headed, fair-skinned Irish guy from the south side of Chicago), worked as a hairdresser to and courted several Playboy bunnies, rubbed elbows with mobsters of the Chicago Outfit, instigated the now-infamous Chicago "dojo war" that took the life of his best friend James Koncevic on April 23, 1970 and, after a descent into drug and alcohol abuse, died of bleeding ulcers in 1975 at the ripe old age of 36.

Count Dante/John Keehan (left) and his iconic comic book ad (right). Photos courtesy of Floyd Webb.

One may ask, "why in the hell is this crackpot even being discussed here?" For all of Keehan's flaws-and make no mistake there were many-his greatest contribution to the martial arts was his castigation and open contempt for the instructors who relied on mysticism and blind devotion from their students as well as his call for the arts' return to their fighting essence both in the application of their technique and in their proper mindset and attitude.

Page 12 of his aforementioned 1968 booklet has this to say about the latter:

Special note: Proper emphasis on courage, aggressiveness, and actual training hall and street application of *effective* fighting techniques, is the most serious lacking segment in modern day Karate and Gung Fu schools. Many Chinese systems consider courage more important than technique, strength or speed as without it all else fails, and courage can sometimes succeed alone. Most karate schools place little emphasis on courage or "guts fighting" and aggressiveness and usually even frown on it. They also do not permit body contact in their self-defense and sparring practice. This makes for a safe training hall but does little to help develop the body to withstand strike punishment and actually hinders the student when they are forced to use it on the street... Remember, the only true test of a fighting man is what he can do, and no more. Form practice, sparring, self-defense practice and brick breaking are meaningless if the man cannot withstand the burden of the 'real thing'..."

In the October 1976 issue of *Defense Combat* magazine Dante's handpicked successor and protégé William Aguiar further clarified the mental state stressed by Keehan as being a "7 to 10 second drive to the wall, completely going in for one thing and one thing only - to get the opponent down and out and everything over as quickly as possible." Dante's methods emphasized ruthlessness, ferocity and full power attack against your aggressor. Not surprisingly, in an era replete with mystical mumbo-jumbo, this won him few friends and a host of critics. However justified the dislike for Keehan by his contemporaries in other areas may have been, it has been said that progress depends on the unreasonable man and in this respect time has proven the late John Keehan to be a true visionary regarding the reality of self-defense and personal protection.

Another key aspect of proper mental training for self-defense and personal protection involves learning and internalizing a set of 6 training guidelines. These were developed by John Kary USMC (Ret.), founder of the *American Combatives* system of self-defense. A highly decorated United States Marine Corps combat veteran, Kary honed his hand to hand fighting skills in the jungles of Vietnam, saving the life of a South Vietnamese officer and earning the Vietnam Cross of Gallantry. What is remarkable is that he continued to develop his fighting prowess after suffering and recovering from injuries that left him permanently blinded and deaf in one ear. It behooves anyone to listen to what this man has to say and, as such, Mr. Kary's "6 Principles of Combat" have become a staple of our training regimen. Here they are as they are listed in his book, *American Combatives: Devastating Military Self-Defense*:

- **Develop An *OFFENSIVE* Mindset**
- **Trust Your *INSTINCTS***
- **Attack With *RUTHLESSNESS* and *AGGRESSION***
- **Keep Your Attacks *BASIC* and *SIMPLE***
- **Attack *VITAL* Parts Of The Body**
- **Be *CONFIDENT* and *DETERMINED***

Let us now look at each of the 6 Principles in detail. Keep in mind that they are all intrinsically linked together and as such the concepts of each point may overlap. If while reading this section (as well as the rest of the book) you may view certain sections and concepts as redundant, keep this in mind: *Nothing is redundant if it is important.*

Develop An *OFFENSIVE* Mindset

You cannot think of whether or not you will be hurt or injured. You must only think of the total incapacitation, damage and destruction of your attacker. I can guarantee you this, if you are concerned with whether or not you will be hurt, you will attack half-heartedly and without commitment. If you attack that way, guess what? You will be hurt. You need to find whatever "go" button in your brain you have to turn into a horse with blinders. Go on the offense immediately and don't stop until you have succeeded. Bruce Lee's personal philosophy on self-defense is reflected in one of his most famous quotes:

> *"Forget about winning and losing; forget about pride and pain. Let your opponent graze your skin and you smash into his flesh; let him smash into your flesh and you fracture his bones; let him fracture your bones and you take his life! Do not be concerned with escaping safely- lay your life before him!!"*

New Testament verse Luke 17:33 paraphrases this idea:

> *"Whoever tries to keep their life will lose it, and whoever loses their life will preserve it."*

Finally, let's not forget Janis Joplin's famous chorus from her rendition of the famous ballad *Me and Bobby McGee*:

> *"Freedom's just another word for nothin' left to lose..."*

Any way you slice it, you have to let go of everything if you want to save everything. In a dire situation, there's just no other way.

Trust Your *INSTINCTS*
Call it "intuition" or "gut feeling," your instincts are there for a reason. They are there to serve you. If you have a bad feeling about a place or situation, remove yourself from it ASAP. If you have a bad feeling about a particular person, try to put as much distance between you and them as you can. If you feel as though an attack is unavoidable, hit him hard and fast until you can either escape to safety or he is no longer an immediate threat. For a greater discussion of this principle, I highly recommend the best-selling book *The Gift of Fear*, by noted personal security and behavior expert Gavin de Becker. This book does a better job of explaining the principle of instinct and intuition than I ever could and, as such, we will be referencing his work throughout this book.

Attack With *RUTHLESSNESS* and *AGGRESSION*
If you are forced to protect yourself against an attacker, you must attack him with complete viciousness, ruthlessness and unbridled aggression. Your mentality must instantly switch from one of "oh, God, please don't hurt me" to one of "how f**king DARE you attack me?!!" and just as importantly your actions must correspond to that way of thinking. Find whatever motivation you have to. It could be not seeing your children or family again, righteous indignation at someone invading your space, it doesn't matter. Use whatever vehicle you have to in order to plug into the dark side of your nature, and direct those bad intentions on him because I guarantee that's what this sick bastard was planning on doing to you.

Keep Your Attacks *BASIC* and *SIMPLE*
Business models everywhere use the KISS acronym: *Keep It Simple, Stupid* or for you more easily offended types, *Keep it Simple, Silly*. Either way, truer words were never spoken regarding self-defense and personal protection. Several factors play into a real-life encounter. Your adrenaline kicks in, your hands become numb, your breathing increases and gets shallow and rapid. When all of these factors come into play, your ability to pull off complex motions goes right down the john. Your techniques must rely on gross motor skills, period. The *Walking Weapon Self Protection Skills System* employs techniques and principles that are simple to learn, practical to use and effective in real life encounters. Remember the KISS principle, and you will be around to kiss your loved ones goodnight. It's that simple.

Attack *VITAL* Parts Of The Body
What good is an aggressively mounted offense to a non-vital area of the attacker's body? None. Your techniques must be directed at the vital targets of an attacker's body. Remember, all the aggression in the world won't stop a determined attacker unless one of his vital targets are hit; when a vital area is hit with aggression and ruthlessness, your chances of survival become greatly enhanced.

Be *CONFIDENT* and *DETERMINED*
When it comes to defending yourself, all of the previous 5 principles don't mean squat if you are not confident and determined to not only stop your attacker but survive an encounter and get to safety. Often times in just about any type of interpersonal interaction one may hear the phrase, "you're not selling me…" with regards to whether or not someone has gotten their point across. You need to sell yourself on not just the idea that you *can* survive or that

you *may* come out of this, but that you WILL survive and emerge victorious. You need to deep down know that should a situation arise where the use of force is not only necessary but unavoidable that you will inflict damage to your assailant, you will take him out of commission and you will be the one going home in one piece that night. These 6 principles are so woven into all aspects of our training that to try and extract them from the physical aspect of what we do is impossible. As beneficial as it is to read and re-read these (which you should be doing anyway), the only way to really ingrain them into your subconscious is through technique training, which will be discussed in the following chapters.

    The best way to remember and apply all of the 6 principles into one is to adhere to the following statement and treat it as gospel truth. Stick to this and the odds of your survival can only increase.

Bob's
ONE and ONLY
RULE of SELF DEFENSE

To use your closest, most potent weapon against the closest, most vulnerable target of your enemy as swiftly, with as much ruthlessness & aggression and in the most confident and determined manner possible.

CHAPTER 2
PRELIMINARY CONSIDERATIONS

CONCEPT vs. TECHNIQUE

The *Walking Weapon Self Protection Skills System* is a concept-based system, not a technique-based system. Techniques can be changed, adapted and applied depending on the situation, but the concepts never change.

The concepts of our system are based on the Wong Shun Leung system of Wing Chun kung fu. Wing Chun (or as students of the Wong Shun Leung lineage spell it, *Ving Tsun*) is a simple and direct yet precise and sophisticated system of self-defense and personal protection created around 350 to 400 years ago by a diminutive Buddhist nun, Ng Mui. Ng Mui taught her art to a peasant girl, Yim Wing Chun, who successfully applied the art to fend off a much larger male attacker intent on forcing her into marriage. Ng Mui eventually named the art for Yim Wing Chun in recognition of her prowess as a fighter. The art of Wing Chun, while made famous as the art Bruce Lee studied as his only formal martial arts training prior to creating his personal art of *jeet kune do* (the way of the intercepting fist) is ideally suited for anyone seeking simple, direct, efficient and practical tools to use for protection.

Of all of the exponents of the art of Wing Chun, a man named Wong Shun Leung put the art "on the map" so to speak, due to his undefeated record in the notorious bare knuckle, no rules challenge matches on the rooftops of Hong Kong during the 1950's and early 1960's. Wong, himself Bruce Lee's direct instructor under Grandmaster Yip Man, instilled in young Bruce the concepts of no-nonsense personal protection and the idea of making the art work for you and not the other way around. "Be the master, not the slave!" Wong would say when discussing training in Wing Chun, meaning do not try to force yourself to conform to the art but rather make the art work for you. Preferring to view his expression of Wing Chun as a skill set that must constantly be honed and practiced, Wong advocated realism and practicality in training. Given both the history of its' founder and the legendary fighting prowess of Wong Shun Leung- himself only around 5'6" and 140lbs.- it comes as no surprise that the art of Wing Chun is of particular appeal to women, children and those lacking in physical strength. Indeed, the essence of the art is based solely on the concepts of simplicity, efficiency and directness.

While the concepts of the *Walking Weapon Self Protection Skills System* are based on Wing Chun, the techniques themselves have been drawn from various forms of military close quarter combatives. This is not to say that Wing Chun's techniques in and of themselves are ineffective; quite the contrary! However, the techniques of *any* martial art system have little to no value for those unwilling or unable to invest the time to develop them effectively (i.e., the general public and/or non-martial artist). The advantage of drawing techniques primarily from military close quarter combat systems lies in their simplicity, ease with which they are learned, practicality of usage to the most vulnerable areas to an attacker's body and their congruence with the Wing Chun mindset of constant attack against an attacker-in effect, turning the tables on them by becoming proactive, i.e., "protecting" rather than "defending." Ironically, choosing techniques such as these for the reasons just described is in and of itself a very Wing Chun concept. Master Wong Shun Leung encapsulates this marriage of theory and technique when he stated, *"As long as it stays logical, it doesn't matter what you call it or what you're actually doing. If it is logical, if it works, use it! Make the art your slave, and never allow the art to be your master; Wing Chun theory is flawless if you can execute it perfect. But a theory is just a theory, it means nothing if you can't put it to work. You might have a better fighting theory behind your system, but if your skill level is lower than your opponent's skill you'll be easily defeated, all the theory in the world can't save you from losing."* It is from this spirit that this System was born.

Unlike almost every other martial arts or self-defense course out there, we do not try to apply techniques to situations. In the *Walking Weapon System*, the *situation* begets the available *targets*; the *targets* then beget whatever *techniques* are to be used. Think of it this way: if someone chooses to attack me, in doing so he will expose one of his vital targets to me. It is up to me through my training and practice to identify whichever target is most available and respond with the appropriate technique.

By sticking to a core set of techniques and applying those techniques in whatever way the situation calls for, adhering to a never-changing set of concepts and principles with a proactive, aggressive mindset, your odds of surviving a self-defense encounter can only increase.

One final note: you will notice that, aside from the occasional sequences of photos depicting one possible way of stringing techniques together, there are no "self-defense sequences." One must not approach the situation looking for which technique will fit but rather let the situation dictate when, where, if and how each technique should be applied.

4 RANGES OF ANY PHYSICAL ATTACK

In line with our views on standardization and simplicity, we can categorize any physical attack under the sun as falling into one of only 4 categories:

- Kicking
- Punching
- TRAPPING (most lethal range)
- Grappling/Wrestling

Let us look at each of these 4 ranges in detail:

Kicking Range- Kicking range is defined as the extension of the foot. It is the longest range but also the most limited in techniques (i.e., only kicks). See photos below:

Punching Range- Punching range is defined as the extension of the longest range punches (jab or cross). One step in from the kick, it is a shorter range than kicking range but has some kicks available (low line kicks such as shin and knee attacks) See the following photos:

TRAPPING range (note: this is where we live)
Trapping range is defined as one step in from punching range. This is where the most targets are open to us, and it is our heavy artillery comes out. Eye gouges and rakes, head-butting, knees, elbows, etc. Please see below and on following page:

Grappling/Wrestling Range- Grappling/wrestling range is defined as any situation where you are on the ground, either with your assailant or without. See below:

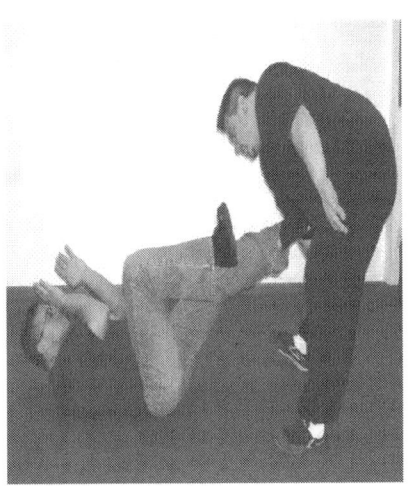 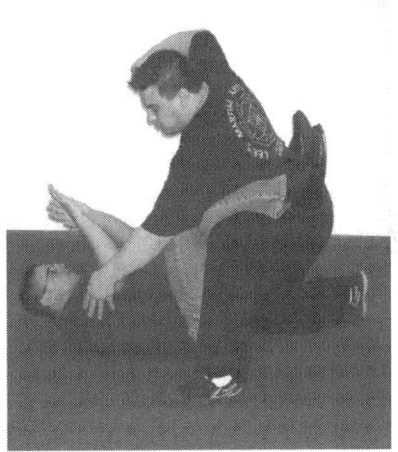

Rather than try to learn ground fighting maneuvers such as armbars, chokes and leg locks one must remember that the vital targets of the body are just as applicable on the horizontal plane (ground, lying down, etc.) as they are on the vertical plane (i.e., standing), as seen in the following photos:

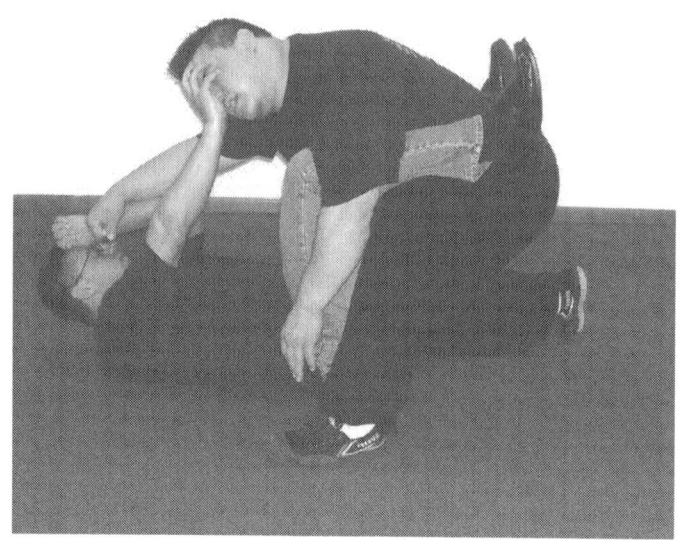

Raking the eyes works on the ground too...

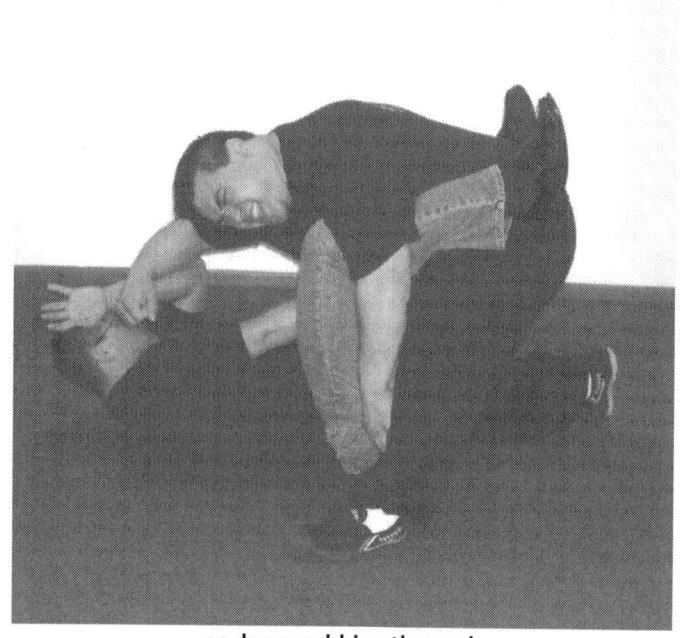

...as does grabbing the groin.

3 FACTORS OF ANY SELF DEFENSE ENCOUNTER

One of the biggest shortcomings in the majority of self-defense systems today is their lack of equally and thoroughly addressing the 3 main factors involved in any altercation. These are:

- **Emotional (before, during and after)**
- **Psychological (before, during and after)**
- **Physical (attack itself and physiological reaction to it-before, during and after)**

EMOTIONAL FACTOR:
This is where people are most often attacked first, many times without knowing it. This manifests itself in the "gut feeling" one gets when in an uncomfortable or unfamiliar environment. Many times you'll hear someone say, "I just have a bad feeling about this place" or words to that effect. This should be your first indicator to increase your awareness, for a bad situation will beget an emotion. As Gavin de Becker states in *The Gift of Fear* (which again I highly recommend you pick up) intuition is your body's finely tuned mechanism of sensing danger. Don't neglect it-it's there to serve you.

Oftentimes you will feel a certain emotion before you formulate a clear thought about why a person, place or situation is cause for concern. To experience the power of emotion, I invite you to try this simple exercise: ask a close friend, sibling, spouse, etc. to get right in your face, eye-to-eye, and hurl insults at you, screaming and staring intently into your eyes like a Drill Instructor. Even though you know in your mind this person is your friend and will never cause you harm, you will feel uncomfortable, your heart rate will increase, you will get fluttery. That is the fight-or-flight response initiating itself, bypassing your mind and activating based solely on your emotional reaction to a perceived threat. *A proper self-protection program can minimize the freeze effect through specific training.* It is noteworthy to mention I used the word *"minimize"* not "eliminate," as well as *"proper"* and *"specific"* to describe the method. In my experience I have found the most valuable training device for conditioning the body to react is a process known as "Adrenal Stress Conditioning." This is a process by which someone is placed in an environment that forces the body into fight-or-flight response through perceived verbal and physical abuse, while in a safe and controlled environment. An excellent example of Adrenal Stress Conditioning can be seen in any basic training component of the military, whereby recruits gradually grow accustomed to the barrage of shouting and intimate face-to-face contact to the point where these actions no longer phase them and they are able to think and react clearly, devoid of distraction. That ability to function under duress with a calculating mindset is what one must incorporate into their personal protection program if one expects to call upon these skills should they ever be needed.

PSYCHOLOGICAL FACTOR

How many times have you practiced a certain skill but were unable to grasp it? The harder you tried, the harder it was to perform this skill, until finally you just didn't care anymore-and then BAM! You performed that very same skill flawlessly and with ease? *Once you stopped thinking about it and turned off the mind chatter the skill became much simpler.* Learning to bypass the "thought process" is what we are attempting to do here.

In my experience I have found that the overwhelming majority of self-defense, personal security, etc., courses fall short because they tend to make *too many presuppositions*, which is without a doubt a BAD thing. For example, the techniques taught for the most part tend to be very attack-specific, which presupposes that an attacker will approach you in a *certain* way, with a *certain* technique, coming at you from a *certain* angle. Another assumption made is the environment in which you will be attacked. Anyone who doubts this statement need only drop by any "self-defense" course being taught at a local martial arts school. I'll bet you 10 dollars you'll most likely see people barefoot, wearing pajama-like uniforms practicing intricate multiple-move techniques against very specific attacks in a clean, spacious studio with wide open spaces in which to practice. Does that sound realistic to you? Me neither-but more on that later. Perhaps the most dangerous assumption made (unbeknownst to them) by many students of martial arts is to *presuppose that the attacker has a similar set of values as they do.* This is due to the fact that teaching students restraint in their techniques while in a psychologically and emotionally stable environment has no element of reality, and as such, the reality of the situation, i.e., that whoever is attacking you has different values to begin with because, well, they're attacking you for no reason, is simply not a valid issue.

One factor many overlook is how the Psychological Factor is very closely linked to the Emotional factor, The Emotional to the Physical, and the Physical to the Psychological. By that I mean *a change in one will always elicit a change in at least one of the other two.* Think of a time when you were nervous or scared. It could be the first time you asked someone out on a date, waiting for medical testing results, anything stressful. Remember that event, really try to get back into the mindset you had, what you were thinking....now how do you feel? I'll bet you have an increased heart rate, pulse, and rate of breathing. Even though you were physically far removed from the stressful situation and in no immediate danger whatsoever, intently focusing on and thinking about a stressful or traumatic event elicited a particular emotional response, which manifested itself in certain physical characteristics. Inversely, having the "gut feeling" we described earlier will get your mind working overtime, you will begin to over-analyze situations, thereby causing yourself more emotional angst which in turn will affect your pulse, breathing, etc. Hopefully by now you're beginning to see just how interrelated the Emotional, Psychological and Physical aspects of any situation are, and self-defense training is no different. In fact, it is only when one can effectively manage these three aspects of their self-defense training that one can begin to obtain that sense of confidence and inner peace that so many martial artists strive to achieve, or say they've achieved but have not.

Proper training, in order for it to be effective, must address certain points. For example, one must be made aware of legalities and be conditioned to react when necessary. Techniques such as verbal diffusion of a particular threat, rationalization, and the concept of de-valuing yourself in the eyes of your attacker should be taught and implemented into scenario response training. Remember, in a self-defense situation, Murphy's Law will undoubtedly come into play, so the less mind-clutter you have going on the better off you will be, be it techniques or your mind racing through the "what-if?" file cabinet. Proper training can help minimize this aspect as well, so that when faced with a situation, you will be able to respond in a simple, direct and efficient manner and thereby remove yourself from the threat as quickly and with as little effort as possible. In the words of reality self-defense pioneer Tony Blauer, "If you're facing one opponent and you doubt yourself, you're outnumbered." Wise words, indeed.

PHYSICAL FACTOR
The Physical factor is the most-often focused on aspect of self-defense. This is understandable, as one obviously needs to learn specific techniques and be able to execute them effectively. I am not implying that the Physical aspect of self-defense training is the least important, quite the contrary. A baseline level of physical prowess is essential for the successful execution of self-defense techniques, HOWEVER, the majority of techniques being taught under the guise of self-defense are ineffective at best, downright dangerous at worst. Here are some of the most common flaws in physical techniques:

Too scenario-specific, i.e., "If someone grabs you HERE then you do THIS....if someone grabs you THERE then you do THAT."

Too many sequences per self-defense technique-
Example: "Against a wrist grab, do this...and then this...and then this..."

Training does not include an element of danger
If scenario training has no intensity to it, it has little value for ingraining proper response.

Emphasis on unrealistic/sport techniques for self-defense
I remember being in a style relying heavily on kicks, and for self-defense training we were doing classical forearm blocks with high side kicks against an armed attacker! Call me overly analytical but I had my doubts even then as to how well my mother would be able to incapacitate an attacker if she were forced to use this.

A lack of a physical fitness regimen
We're not talking hardcore workout here, but a basic fitness regimen has no negative side effects as far as self-defense is concerned.

Improper mindset while training
Last, but certainly not least, the emphasis on all too many courses is one of a "reactionary" mindset, rather than a "proactive" one. More on this will be discussed when techniques are introduced, however, this goes hand in hand with the aforementioned principle of attack-specific scenarios-i.e., don't wait for someone to grab your wrist before you decide to be proactive about improving your situation! In order to rectify this situation, proper training must do the following:

- Techniques must be simple, relying on gross motor skills
- Techniques must be direct and economical, focusing on the body's 3 main target areas: eyes, throat and groin
- Techniques must be able to be used by anyone, regardless of size or physical strength

So, knowing what we know now about the 3 factors in self-defense situations, here's a pop quiz for you: why is it not a good idea to rely on long-sequences or complicated moves? Answer: because Murphy's Law is a real bitch and she likes to come out and play at the worst possible time.

Remember our mantra: *"the LESS you have to remember, the MORE you have to work with."*

"Be peaceful, be courteous, obey the law, respect everyone; but if someone puts his hand on you, send him to the cemetery."
-Malcolm X

"A tornado haze of windmill violence...brutal defeats refined; simple dominates complicated."
-Frank Woolsey

2 TYPES OF ATTACKERS

The mentality of an attacker can generally be classified into two categories:

Territorial
Sociopathic

The *territorial* attacker will generally diffuse the attack once you remove yourself from the area. This can be seen more often with men marking their territory on a corner, a park, wherever they mark as their "turf." A territorial attacker situation will generally sound something like this:

"Hey, you!!
What the fuck you think you're doing around here?
You want some of this??
No?
Yeah, you better keep walkin,' bitch!
You don't want none of this!"

Once the "threat" to their pride and status is removed, their hostility drops. The *sociopathic* attacker is infinitely more dangerous, as the sociopathic attacker has made up his mind to attack you no matter what you do, either after confronting you in a similar manner as is listed above or without prior warning.

In either scenario, if you square off, holding your fists up and spout obscenities back to him, his awareness will (either consciously or subconsciously) rise to a higher level, as in "this guy/girl knows something, I have to be a little more aware." By keeping yourself in a non-aggressive posture while using verbal diffusion techniques all without sounding or appearing timid or afraid (as this will almost guarantee them attacking you), you put yourself in a much more effective position to successfully protect yourself and take the bad guy out of commission. Use common sense. If a mugger stands ten feet away with a gun, the guy's a pro-give him what he wants UNLESS he tells you to get in a car or follow him somewhere-because then you're going to Crime Scene B.

Crime Scene B
There are two crime scenes-Crime Scene A, where the crime takes place, and Crime Scene B-where they find the victim's body. If anyone ever tells you to get in a car, doorway, etc., DO NOT DO IT. Personally, my mentality is this: If you ask me for my wallet, jacket or whatever, no problem. Here, take it. Have a great day. If I give you my wallet or jacket or whatever...and you still want me to come with you, at that point I know I only have two options:

Option A: I can go with you and watch my odds of survival drop to ZERO

or

Option B: I launch a full blown offense against you, going for your eyes, throat and balls, which gives me a 50/50 chance.

Now I was never a Mathlete in high school but I do know that in terms of survival, 50% is one hell of a lot better than 0%. A bit black-and-white an outlook, perhaps, but listen to the radio or watch the news for 5 minutes and you will see this is a pretty twisted world we live in and the reality is that bad things happen every day.

You can either choose to accept the way the world works and realistically address the situation, or you can pretend it doesn't exist and watch the latest episode of whatever reality television show the powers-that-be have concocted to further dumb down the masses and herd them like sheep. Choose wisely, and remember the following phrase:

Casus Belli:
An act or event that provokes or justifies war

That is what it is going to boil down to should you be attacked. If someone attacks you for no reason, they have just declared war against you. Remember, British Prime Minister Neville Chamberlain tried to appease Adolf Hitler for years to stave off war, but when Hitler rolled his tanks into Poland that day in 1939, there was no doubt anymore. Verbal diffusion, de-escalation or removing yourself from a bad situation is all preferable to direct conflict, but if that should occur, you shouldn't question someone's intentions at that point; they are very clear. They want to hurt you. Their attack has become your *casus belli*. Respond accordingly.

CASUS BELLI

2 CATEGORIES OF ANY PHYSICAL ATTACK

Regardless of scenario specifics, any attack one may find oneself faced with must fall into one of only 2 broad categories:

You see it coming
You don't see it coming

As the dynamics of each category are different, they will be addressed separately.

Attacks you see coming
In line with our concept of simplification, we want to get away from the idea of being *attack-specific*, i.e., against a left-leg kick do this, against a right-handed hooking punch do this - wrong, wrong, WRONG!! This leads to mind clutter and ultimate paralysis by analysis. A much more effective and efficient method of dealing with an assailant's attack is to learn to identify an attack by the angle from which it comes in.
Regardless of specific targets, weapons (fist, foot, club, etc.), all attacks you can see coming must fall into one of two categories: LINEAR or CIRCULAR.

Examples of Linear Attacks include:
Straight punches (jab/cross)
Front or side kick
Knee
Bull rush / tackle
"Frankenstein" Choke (one or two handed from the front)
Push/shove

Examples of Circular Attacks include:
Overhand punches
Uppercuts
Hooks
Roundhouse kicks
Any swinging attack, empty handed or with weapons

When you can read an attack by angles, now you only have two general attacks to defend against, not two hundred.

Attacks you don't see coming
Attacks you don't see coming are fundamentally different from those you can, not only in technique but also in situation. Attacks you can see coming are usually frontal, while attacks you can't see coming are mostly from the sides or rear. Attacks you can see coming are often preceded by verbal or nonverbal cues such as "hard looks," yelling, trash-talking, posturing, etc. Those cues allow you the opportunity to intercept the attack verbally attempting to diffuse the situation or intercept the attack with an attack of your own. Attacks you don't see coming oftentimes contain none of these cues and are referred to as "sucker punch" attacks or ambushes for just this reason. Our reaction to such attacks requires a higher degree of sensitivity and awareness and, as such, require specific scenario training to prepare for.

Examples of Attacks you don't see coming:

Grabs
Chokes (especially from the side or from behind)
Sucker punches
Bull-rushes
Side/ rear tackles, side headlocks, etc.

VITAL TARGETS

The vital targets on the body can be classified in two categories: *primary* and *secondary*.

Primary Targets (3)
As we briefly touched on earlier, the core of this system is comprised of gross motor skill techniques designed to take anyone out of commission by attacking the three primary targets on the body. These are:

EYES   THROAT   GROIN

Why do we focus on these areas?
They render size and strength irrelevant- Everyone will react the same when hit in the groin, poked in the eye or jabbed in the throat. It is for this reason that these targets are known as "equalizers."
They are equally damaging on the vertical and horizontal plane- For example, a kick to the groin or thumb to the eyeball while standing will elicit the same reaction, i.e., incapacitation, as a palm to the groin will while on the ground.
They require comparatively little pressure or strength- This is what makes this system so effective and adaptable for women, the physically small or elderly, and children learning to deal with potential attackers, "stranger danger," etc.
Hitting any one of these targets has an instantaneous effect: PAIN- For example, a 6'3" 220lb. heavyweight boxer can absorb round after round of abuse to his head and body, but will be unable to withstand abuse to the groin or eyes. This "stopping power" creates options for you to remove yourself as quickly as possible from the situation.

Secondary Targets (9+)

In addition to the 3 vital targets there are several secondary targets on which we can inflict much collateral damage, and can aid in opening up a line of attack to one of our primary targets. These are listed below:

Ears
Sides and Back of Neck
Jaw
Solar Plexus
Collarbone
Bladder / Pubic Area
Knees
Shins
Instep/Top of Foot/Toes
Any other vulnerable target on opponent's body (situational)

Remember, there will always be at least one secondary target available any time an assailant encroaches your personal space since in order to do so he will be venturing into one of the 4 Ranges of Combat previously discussed.

"When self defense becomes complicated, it is no longer self defense."
-R. Hoover

PRIMARY STANCES (4)

The *Walking Weapon Self Protection Skills System* uses 4 primary stances. They are:

- Non-Aggressive Ready Stance
- Folded Arm Stance
- Thinker / Jack Benny Stance
- Neutral Stance

The stance you will use depends on several factors- your environment, whether the attack is one you can see coming (and thereby try to avoid or diffuse) or not, your body posture at that exact moment, and so on. Since no amount of planning can adequately address any contingency you may find yourself in, our stances need to be natural, adaptable and versatile.

The stance most often referenced in this book will be the first one covered in this section, which we call the Non-Aggressive Ready Stance. Obviously if one is ambushed or sucker punched or if the attack is a sudden grab, choke or tackle this stance is not ideal. However, just as a baby must learn to crawl before walking, we need a stance to train in that allows us the opportunity to practice each technique in such a manner that the technique itself can be grasped and internalized with as little variation as possible. After training in this manner and gaining familiarity with the technique itself, one can then integrate variables that will necessitate different stances. Once the technique is ingrained and the dynamics of each stance are grasped, then it's "game on" and the real fun begins in training.

NON-AGGRESSIVE READY STANCE

"Do not become tense, but ready..." Bruce Lee

From here the defender can react in any number of ways.

The "non-aggressive ready stance" derives its name from the notion that to an attacker or an observer of the altercation you appear timid, non-threatening and, as the name clearly states, non-aggressive. Some key points to this stance:
- Feet are 1-1.5 steps apart
- Front foot is pointed forward, aiming at target/aggressor
- Rear foot is 60-90 degrees perpendicular to front foot
- Ideal weight distribution is 50/50
- Hips slightly turned inward, taking the groin off of centerline
- Elbows in close to body
- Hands-up (chin level), open and facing outward

FEET- The feet are 1 to 1.5 steps apart-this is wide enough to offer stability but also narrow enough to permit mobility, either forwards and backwards or laterally. Many traditional arts place much emphasis on deep, rooted stances. While this is a superb leg workout, as well as a very stable position, it offers little in the way of mobility and fluidity-two factors essential to survival in any self-defense encounter. The toe of the front foot points towards your target/opponent, while the rear foot angles off anywhere from 60 to 90 degrees. These are not exact, etched-in-stone figures; it's not like you have to look down at your feet while preparing to protect yourself and say, "Well now, let me see...are my feet angled between 45 and 90 degrees? No? Well, I had better change them...hold on a second Mr. Rapist-Ah... there we are...." This is a fluid stance and as such relies on flexible and adaptive footwork. The main reasons for the rear foot being angled outward are balance and removing your groin off of the centerline.

WEIGHT DISTRIBUTION- Weight distribution should be approximately 50% on the front leg and 50% on the rear leg. This ensures that a sudden change in position will not place you off balance. You should not be flat footed but rest the majority of your weight on the balls of your feet, while keeping your heel as flat as possible. This masks your intent to take action and creates the image of not being able to assert yourself to your attacker.

HIPS- The hips are rotated slightly inward, that is to say, towards the direction of the rear foot. This removes the groin from being directly squared up to the assailant as well as making a lunging attack requiring both of the assailant's hands shooting forward simultaneously such as a grab, choke or tackle a bit more difficult to execute as well as making one's defense against such an attack more efficient.

ELBOW PLACEMENT- Elbows are in towards the body, more towards the front as opposed to the sides-this will aid in the forward pressure of the techniques taught later in this course. Also, by placing your elbows more towards the front, it will be more difficult to trap your arms at your sides should you be bear-hugged or body-locked. The elbows remain tight to prevent an opponent getting his under-hooks in on you, thereby making it one hell of a lot easier to pick you up and slam you into next week. More on this principle will be covered in the next section.

HANDS- Hands should be three things: up, open and facing outward.
Your hands should be up at chin level: This ensures they can be used both offensively and defensively based on what the situation alls for.
Your hands should be open: Do NOT make fists- this signals to your attacker that you are preparing to take some form of retaliatory action in this encounter, which in turn, will make him raise either consciously or subconsciously raise his awareness level.
Your palms should be facing outward: The placement of the hands palms out "seals the deal," so to speak, for selling him the idea that you are passive and non-threatening, although you have just placed yourself in a very advantageous position as far as the opportunities afforded you for either evasion, blocking or attacking. The idea of this stance is to present the idea to your attacker that you are timid, non-aggressive and for all intents and purposes an easy target. This stance is also accompanied by verbal diffusion techniques such as:

- "Hey man, I don't want any trouble okay?"
- If I did something to piss you off I apologize"
- "Hey, look man-let's all just calm down, okay?"

Now let's assume for a moment that you're a would-be attacker. You instigate a confrontation and your "victim" reacts by putting his/her hands up, slightly stepping back all the while saying, "Listen, man, I don't want any problems here-I mean, if I did something to piss you off I apologize..."

Notice how the defender is like a coiled spring; ready to react.

You continue forward; smirking at the piece of easy prey in front of you, while cocking back to fire a hook to take their head off...

WHAM!

They slam a palm to your face, and follow with a knee to your groin, leaving you on the ground in the fetal position while they promptly get the hell out of there. Meanwhile, you're left wondering what just happened to you. That's the *Walking Weapon Self-Protection Skills System* in a nutshell.

FOLDED ARM STANCE

Photo courtesy of the Author.

The folded-arm stance is another example of using non-threatening posture to secretly place yourself in an advantageous position, although the main advantage to training this stance stems from the fact that it is a posture which damn near everyone uses every single day. Note how in the picture the body is angled away-this takes the vital targets off of the centerline. The hands can shoot forward to react and defend oneself or proactively intercept and attack an assailant should they venture too close into one's personal space (i.e., the moment one is inside kicking range).

THINKER / JACK BENNY STANCE

Photos courtesy of Auguste Rodin Gallery (left) and Gutterfighting USA website (right).

    This stance draws its name from the above 2 photographs: The world-renowned bronze sculpture titled *The Thinker*, by Auguste Rodin (left), and famous comedian Jack Benny, who would often deliver the monologues for his variety show standing in this very posture (right). Note the posturing of the body in both cases: one hand is up, stroking or placed gently under the chin, while the opposite arm is folded across the midsection or chest. Several close quarter systems use this stance for good reason: this posture is useful for both defense against any surprise attack, sucker punch, etc., as well as launching an attack of your own when no other course of action will do.

This stance appears laid back, relaxed and quite harmless but it places your hands in a good position to strike quickly and defend against any attack if necessary.

The hand on the chin can also be used as a distraction if it is moved around while talking and attempting to verbally diffuse the situation yet poised to lash out as soon as a threat is imminent.

"No intelligent man has ever lost a fight to someone who said, 'I'm gonna kick your ass.'"
-Rory Miller

NEUTRAL STANCE

"Maybe I'll pick up a beef sandwich and-...uh-oh..."

    The Neutral Stance can best be summed up in one word-Natural. Your hands are down, your weight can either be shifting from one foot to the other or straight on 50-50. Think of any time you are waiting in line for anything. The purpose of training this stance is to train to react quickly any time you are caught off guard in a surprise attack scenario. Remember that in training this stance, one must de-focus and wait for the attack to come in before reacting even if he/she can see the attack coming in training, because that's the whole idea: reacting to an ambush, sucker punch or sudden attack. Don't wait for it; just think about something else. Be genuinely surprised when it comes-that's exactly the feeling we're looking to generate.

Note that for all 4 stances, the all aspects of the footwork as listed in the breakdown of the Non-Aggressive Ready Stance (feet placement, weight distribution, balance and shifting) apply. Refresh those key points and apply them to all 4 stances in your training. Specific training drills for each stance will be discussed in greater detail in both *Chapter 5: Extreme Situations and Weapons Training* as well as *Chapter 6: Training Progression & Recommended Equipment*. After reading each of those chapters, do yourself a solid and go back to this section to refresh the specifics of each of these stances.

A NOTE ON "VERBAL JUDO"
DIFFUSING CONFLICTS THROUGH LANGUAGE

The importance of using of verbal diffusion techniques to either de-escalate a potentially harmful situation before it begins or portray a sense of helplessness to give the attacker a momentary sense of overconfidence before you launch a pre-emptive strike if an attack is inevitable cannot be over-emphasized. This skill, one of using words to subtly negotiate outcomes in one's favor, has masterfully articulated by George J. Thompson, PhD., and Jerry B. Jenkins in their book *Verbal Judo: The Gentle Art of Persuasion*. The title is based on the fact that Judo (literally translated as "gente way") is a martial art devoid of strikes and entirely based on using one's force against him/herself via throwing motions. The book itself covers far too much material to paraphrase here but for our specific purposes verbal diffusion can best be summarized in one word: *empathy*. Apologizing for any perceived slight or act of disrespect such as passing through one's "turf" or territory, accidentally giving someone a longer than passing stare or just plain stating something to the effect of "if I did anything to piss you off I apologize," may just mean the difference between walking away from a conflict having just stroked the would-be assailant's ego and having to drive your thumbs into someone's eyes and possibly deal with the legal ramifications of that act, however justified, for a long time (although I would always prefer to be tried by 12 than carried by 6). If all they're after is you acting meek so they can strut their peacock tailfeathers, fine. If they want to do you in, you can create an illusion of timidity that may just buy you a sceond or two to launch your ruthless attack.

> "Everybody's got a plan until they get smacked in the face."
> -Mike Tyson

CHAPTER 3
UPPER BODY TECHNIQUES AND STRATEGIES

Upper Body Technique # 1: EVASION/PARRY

Note the body cohesion and rotation from the waist.

    The first technique in this system isn't necessarily a technique *per se*, in the sense of a weapon, but more of an entry into the other techniques. The parry/evasion is a situational technique. For example, if your best friend or brother-in-law is drunk and becoming belligerent, and you wish to restrain him but he is starting to get rowdy and there's a chance of you sustaining some physical injury, then this comes into play. When you are unsure as to what course of action to take and need a second to assess the situation but still require protective ability, this also is when you use this technique. And, if ever you should find yourself facing an attacker, this is an invaluable way to gauge factors like distance and the attacker's reach while maintaining your personal space and providing a barrier.

MECHANICS

As the strike/shove/choke comes forward, use the forearm of whatever side mirrors the side from which the attack comes from to deflect (Example: in a left lead stance, against an attack from what would be your left side, use your left forearm/hand to parry while pivoting counterclockwise on your left foot and moving your right foot). Be sure to use footwork to add power to the deflection as well as removing your body out of the trajectory of the incoming attack. Also, maintain the proper positioning of your elbows (in towards body). See accompanying photos.

Note the opposite hand up guarding the centerline.

Some tips on body positioning to perform this correctly and efficiently:
- Never cross your centerline with your hands or arms
- Move from your waist to deflect incoming blows
- Use proper footwork to turn your body as a whole

A parry with the lead hand:

The defender isn't swatting the hand away; he is guiding it past him, thereby diffusing pressure while maintaining his structure.

And with the rear hand:

Another view of the previous commentary.

Note: the evasion/parry works to deflect an oncoming linear attack. Any circular attack can best be diffused by cutting off the opponent at the base of his power, i.e., his torso (which we will see next).

Upper Body Technique # 2: ICEBREAKER / COW-CATCHER

This technique goes by various names. We call it an Ice Breaker or a Cow-Catcher due to the similarity in structure and function of the ice breaker on the bow of a ship in the Arctic or the old cow-catchers on the front of locomotives that would force cattle off the railroad tracks in the days of the Old West. Whatever the nickname, the general premise is the same: to intercept any circular attack by jamming the opponent, at his power base. Question: would you rather get hit by a baseball bat while standing six inches from your opponent or 4 feet away? If you answered 4 feet I know a great chiropractor. High school physics teaches us that the farther away from a swinging object you are, the more time it has to build up centrifugal force, thereby causing a much more devastating blow.

     Have you ever been sitting watching TV and suddenly a car backfires, a door slams because of the wind or my personal favorite-jumping out at someone when they walk through the front door? Everyone in the world flinches. It's a natural response. What this "cow-catcher" principle does is mimic that response into a technique that allows you to bridge the gap from the danger zone, i.e., long-range, kick and punch territory, to what is known as trapping range, the range where your natural weapons (elbows, knees, eye-rakes, shin scrapes and stomps, etc.) can come into play and where your 4 main targets are at your disposal. This technique can be seen in several Southeast Asian arts, such as the Indonesian art of *pentjak silat* (which is where the Author was first exposed to it) which call it a "dive entry." One training methodology, in fact, is created entirely around this technique. Reality based self-defense pioneer Tony Blauer, founder of Blauer Tactical Systems, has built an entire system around this concept which he has termed the S.P.E.A.R. System, an acronym for *S*pontaneous *P*rotection *E*nabling *A*ccelerated *R*esponse.

MECHANICS
From your Non-Aggressive Ready Stance, simply sink your weight down and burst forward while shooting your arms out towards whatever shoulder the strike originates from, while keeping those elbows bent. This is imperative. If you allow your arms to straighten out, any reactive capability you have is now gone because you have now over-committed yourself. Also, your sides are now exposed to either attacks to the flank (side) or being bear-hugged.

Observe the following photos:

Note the drive from the rear heel through the legs, hips and out the arms.

Another point that cannot be overstressed is to keep your chin tucked towards your chest and look forward from the tops of your eyes, like you're diving into a pool (hence the term *dive entry*). This creates a natural shield for your jaw with your shoulders against hooking punches and swinging attacks. With slight adjustment, this technique/concept also works like a dream against the good ol' fashioned bull rush/tackle-just drop your center of gravity (hips) lower than you would against a punch. As you drop, simultaneously stick your butt out as you thrust your forearms into his neck or shoulder. This position will lend itself nicely to the knee, as we will see later in Chapter 4. *Note: You don't need to know what attack is coming to bust this one out.* That's what makes this technique so versatile and so usable. Not only does it serve to intercept an attack, but it also places you in the position to tee off on your opponent's vital areas while simultaneously taking you out of your opponent's power wheelhouse... As an added bonus, as you shoot your arms forward, the angle and position of your inside forearm makes it very compatible with smashing into the assailant's face, either in the throat, chin or nose.

POINTS TO REMEMBER FOR THE ICE BREAKER / COW-CATCHER
- Sink your weight before you propel forward
- Keep your elbows in even as you shoot your arms forward-this helps guard your flank (side) from attacks and prevents being bear-hugged
- Keep your chin tucked and your eyes looking forward through the top of your eyes like you're diving into a pool
- Do NOT fully extend your arms-you should still have some bend in them even after making contact

with the assailant's body-this ensures that you are still close enough to not get hit by any telling blows, the way you would if you were in punching range. Also if you extend your arms, there is a chance the attackers arms can "ride" yours into your body, creating a grappling situation and opening up a whole other can of worms that one does not want opened in a self-defense scenario.

An example against an attack to the defender's left side:

And against an attack to the defender's right side:

Note in the previous photo sequence as the assailant comes forward, the defender's hands instinctively come up and his back "turtles up" as his shoulders shrug, protecting his neck. As the elbows shoot forward and the weight is sunk to the heels, this creates a driving force which begins with the heels and ends with wherever the forearms make contact with the assailant-in this case, flush with the side of the neck. In certain cases, if the side of the neck is hit just right, blood flow to the carotid artery (which delivers oxygenated blood to the brain) is interrupted, resulting in what is called a "flash knockout." It is in cases like this that the attacker literally runs into the defender's forearms much the same as if he were to walk straight into a wall.

There is no subsitute for actual training to develop the sensitivity of knowing when and how to apply this technique. The good news is that as stated before this is a natural reaction that, with training, you can make work for you. Just get out there and practice, practice, practice!

"In any moment of decision, the best thing you can do is the right thing, the next best thing is the wrong thing, and the worst thing you can do is nothing."
-Teddy Roosevelt

Upper Body Technique # 3: EYEJAB

As soon as you detect any movement towards you...strike!

    This particular technique is used as an interception to any type of forward attack or looping hand strike. Often times, martial art systems overload their practitioners by presenting different defenses for various specific attacks. This "attack-specific" defense is dangerous-remember what I stated earlier, "The LESS you have to remember, the MORE you have to work with." Against any hooking attack, be it an overhand, a wild, looping long-range uppercut (why someone would throw a long range uppercut is anybody's guess but hey, I've seen weirder) or a John Wayne haymaker hook, an eye-jab flicked straight out will neutralize the attack and provide you with the opportunity to either take the attacker out of commission or get out of there.

NOTE: Techniques like these are what are called "stun and run" techniques. You will most likely NOT defeat someone with an eye-jab alone (although that is the best-case scenario). What you will do is give yourself options to either follow up to one of his other primary targets to take him out of commission or leave him incapacitated long enough to get the hell out of there.

MECHANICS

To perform the eye-jab correctly, bunch your fingers together and flick your hand out in a loose (but not too loose) whipping motion directed at one of your opponent's eyes. Think of trying to tap an elevator button with your fingertips. Use shuffle step-footwork (which will be covered in detail in the next Chapter) similar to the Ice-Breaker/Cow-Catcher to move into your attack, this will put you out of your opponent's "wheelhouse" of power-remember the baseball bat analogy?

Practice the eye-jab in a mirror, first stationary then moving around and eventually with a partner. Your partner can hold his/her hand up or wear a focus pad or goggles. You want to progress to the point where you can sense an attack coming and intercept it with an offensive attack of your own. Refer to Chapter 6 for proper training progression methodologies.

This technique can be trained in the mirror or any type of punching bag apparatus, such as the BOB (Body Opponent Bag), as seen in the following photo, for more realism, as it has facial features such as cheekbones, eyes and a nose.

Don't take the following sequence (or any other sequence in this book, for that matter) as a step-by-step guide; just know that this is just one option of what it looks like when properly done. Think of these techniques as letters, from which you can learn to spell words (combinations) and eventually formulate those words into sentences (self-protection, escaping a rape attempt, etc.) removing yourself from harm.

Trying to verbally diffuse and talk my way out of it...

but I see the hand cock back, so I hit first!

74

As he recoils from the stun and my forward pressure...

I land a knee to his belly or his groin based on availability...

...and call it a day with an elbow shot to his temple.

"*Si Vis Pacem, Para Bellum*"
(translation)
"*If you want peace, prepare for war.*"

-Publius Flavius Vegetius Renatus

Upper Body Technique # 4: EYE RAKE

"His hands can't hit what his eyes can't see..." Muhammad Ali

    Attacking an assailant's eyes will almost certainly take him out of commission. The following personal anecdote illustrates my point: Once, a training partner of mine and I were sparring hard for an upcoming tournament. We were really laying into each other, giving and taking one hell of a beating but we kept going. We were strong, conditioned and ready to kick ass. Suddenly, he flicked out a back-fist strike which I weaved to avoid, but his fingertips accidentally swiped my eye. Instantly I dropped to my knees and clutched at my face. I was completely helpless, when two seconds before I was pumped up and ready to go. That is how potent a strike like this can be and just think...that was from a light brush with the fingers! Lesson here: do NOT underestimate the power of attacking the eyes.

MECHANICS
The eye rake can be done either single or double-handed. To perform the single hand eye rake correctly, fashion your hand in a claw, as if you are gripping the end of a dumbbell

Tear down the opponent's face, slicing his eyes with your nails.

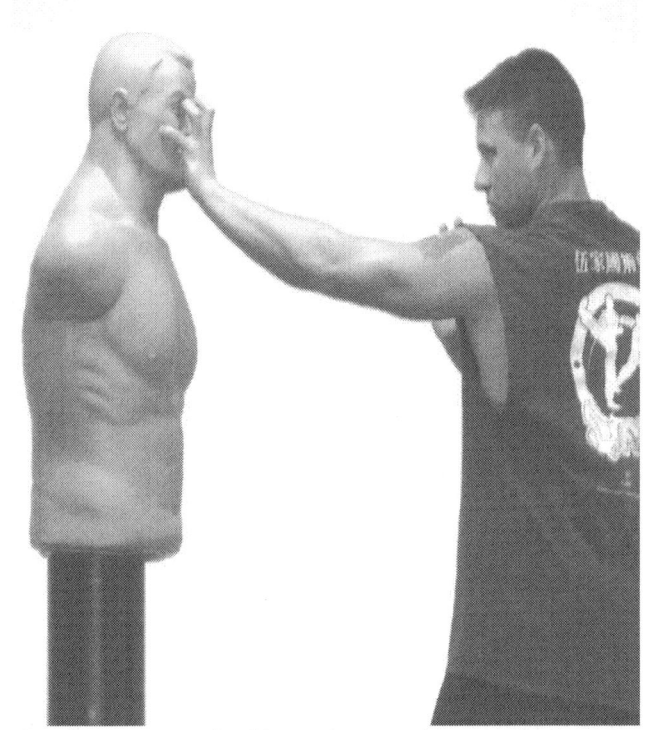

You have to put some bad intentions on this attack. Get primal!!

This can also be applied quite effectively in conjunction with Upper Body Technique # 6-the Chin Jab which will be discussed further in this book as the trajectories are complementary: up with the chin jab, down with the eye rake.

Another very effective manner of using the eye rake is a double-handed eye rake. To perform the double handed eye rake one must be in trapping range (again, where you are inside of punching and kicking range), since this is where you can do the most damage and are also safest from most hard strikes, kicks, haymaker punches, etc.

Refer to the following photos:

Drive from the heels and propel your energy forward.

Thrust out from the elbows as you drive the thumbs into the assailant's eyes, burying them into the sockets or raking the eyes with the thumbs, tearing out and back (as seen above).

Against an assailant it would look more like this:

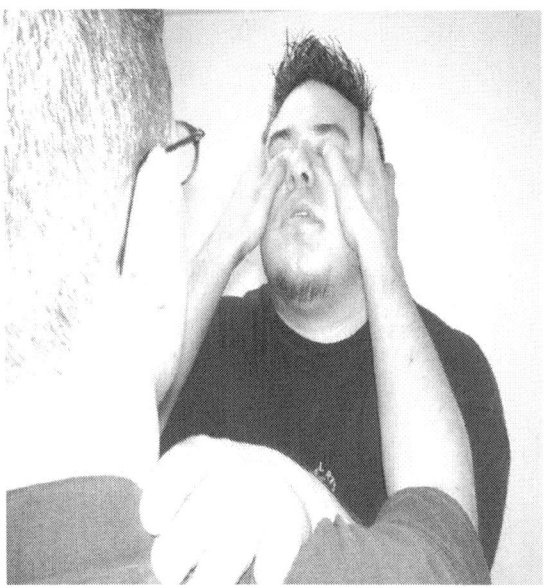

Think, "I'm gonna make this bastard a member of the white cane patrol!"

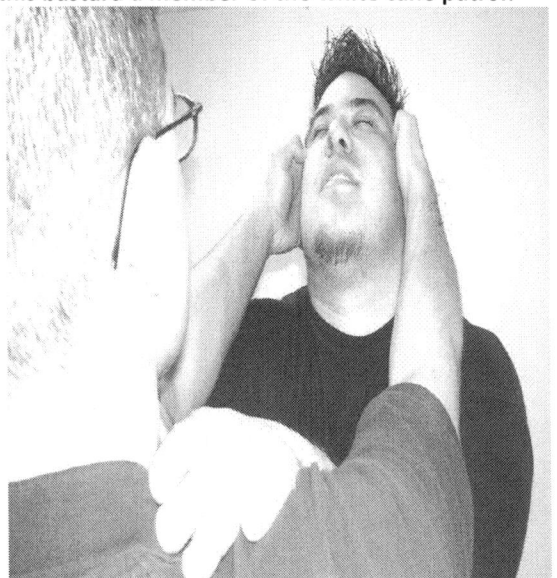

Notice that in the previous sequence that for the sake of safety while training the thumbs have been placed to the side of the eyes but have bent them to show how deeply the thumbs should dig into the eye sockets. Again, the elbows shoot forward and the thumbs drive right into the eyes and tear outward as the pressure continues forward and out the sides. Vicious, I know, but consider the alternative: If this person wants to rape, strangle or defile you and your family, a choice to gouge his eyes isn't a choice at all.

> *"Self defense is recovery from stupidity or bad luck."*
> -Rory Miller

Upper Body Technique # 5: PALM HEEL STRIKE

Note the body unity from the striking hand to the rear heel.

The palm heel strike is in many ways superior for self-defense purposes over a closed fist because a proper punch can sometimes take years to learn and relies heavily on wrist strength for support. Additionally, the palm heel strike allows for greater use of force without risk of injury, since the heel of the palm is one of the most conditioned surfaces on the body-we all use our hands every day-plus we are used to the motion of pushing something with our palm and getting our bodies behind it (think of opening a door or pushing a car).

USES:
The palm heel can be used as an interception, much the same as the eye-jab, although the speed of the eye-jab

makes it a more conducive weapon for interception. It can be delivered with the lead and /or rear hand, as seen in the accompanying photos.

First the lead hand:

Now the rear hand:

Note the power chain from rear heel to striking palm. Against a lunging punch, headlock or bear-hug a palm heel is an ideal technique to use to the attacker's groin. Refer to the following photos:

Refer back to this photo sequence after the footwork section of *Chapter 4*.

The palm heel strike can also be used against a straight attack as a simultaneous parry and hit (this is referred to as a "split sector" attack, since one hand is between the attacker's arms and the other is outside). Note that the defender's other hand is up by the defender's face.

It can also be used against a tackle if caught early enough.

Just make sure your center of gravity is low enough to extend the arm without getting jammed up...otherwise you're in a whole new ball game!

MECHANICS

From your Non-Aggressive Ready Stance, the footwork used in the palm heel strike is identical to that of the eye-jab, you will use your footwork to shuffle in and sink slightly as you make contact with your attacker's face, throat or solar plexus. Your wrist, elbow and shoulder will form a line, known in kinesiology and anatomy circles as a *kinetic chain*. This will allow you to put your body behind the strike and inflict much more damage than just pushing out with your arm. Drive forward with your hips & legs as you strike. Follow up with attacks to the other vital targets. Please reference accompanying photos:

Lead palm heel:

Always remember the hips and legs deliver the power!

Rear hand palm heel:

Note the twist in the body when delivering the rear handed palm heel, much the same way a boxer throws a cross using the hip for rotation.

Upper Body Technique # 6: CHIN JAB

Proof that size and strength don't mean anything when the right target is hit.

For all you history buffs out there, among the many heroes of World War II stood a man named Col. Rex Applegate. Applegate was the trainer of the Allied Forces Commando Units as well as the Office of Strategic Services (OSS), the forerunner to today's CIA. Their hand-to-hand training was done at a secret camp in Canada called Camp X and one of the "bread and butter" techniques of their arsenal was a variation of the palm heel strike known as a *chin jab*. This is a battle-tested technique with roots in the horrors of close-quarter combat. Learn from the heroes of yester-year: Practice this technique until it becomes second nature. It works.

MECHANICS

Fashion the hand as if you are carrying a cantaloupe or large grapefruit. The hand is then driven up from below the chin using not only the arm but also the legs and hips, much the same way a shot put is thrown in the Olympics. If one is close enough to the attacker, the forearm almost rides up the chest. The chest can, in fact, be a useful landmark to apply this technique with in a close-quarters tussle, because if you feel the chest, you know where the head is going to be. This way the defender can ride the chest all the way up to under the chin and, using the hips, legs and arm together, sink the chin jab and knock this sick bastard off his feet and onto the ground.

The following photos were taken during an actual first-time participant learning and applying this technique. Proof that the simpler the technique, the more effective and practical the usage.

Using threatening tone, posture and language...

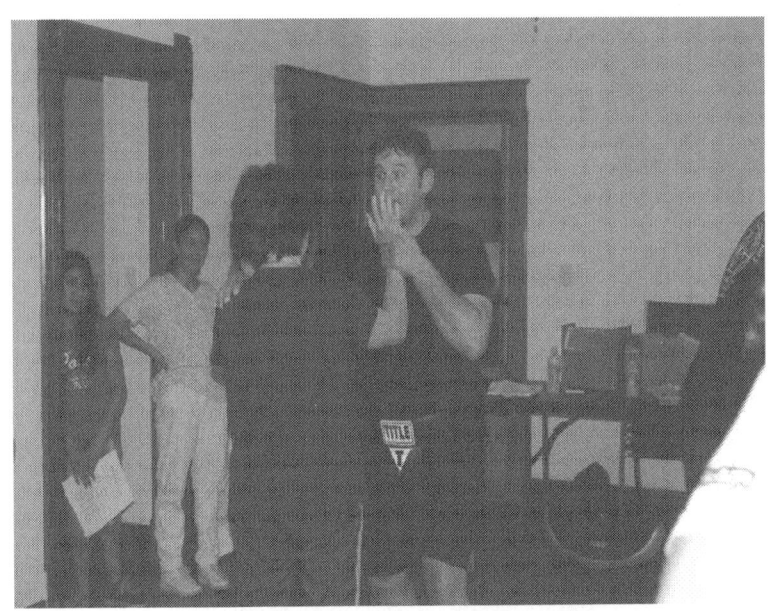

...but once I encroach she attacks me!

Note the proper body unity from rear heel to lead palm.

Once my head is forced back the fingers can easily move downward into the eye rake.

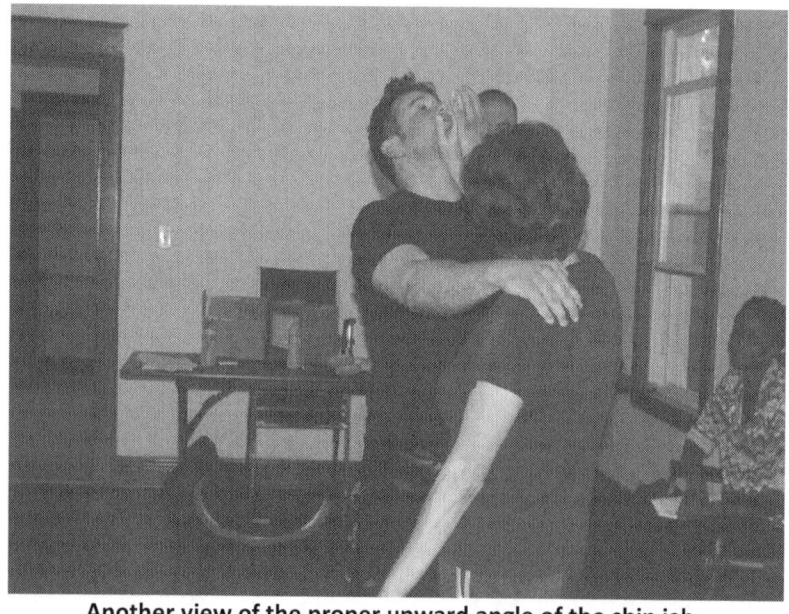

Another view of the proper upward angle of the chin jab.

The following photos illustrate just how the chin cannot resist direct pressure upward. Even after readying the muscles to resist, once the pressure is applied up and in, the muscles of the head and neck simply cannot resist force applied properly and rooted upward from the ground.

Caught by surprise...

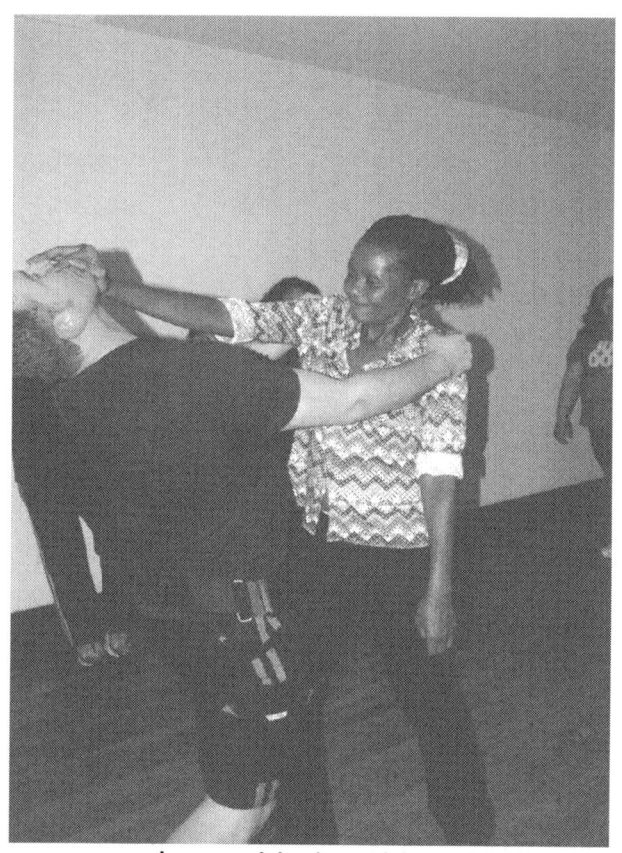

...but not giving in or giving up!

This workshop participant (who, incidentally, had come to the USA from a war-torn and poverty stricken country in Africa and who had never taken a self defense class before in her life) was amazed at how easily and simply she could learn, remember and apply this technique. Note the neutral stance surpirsise attack in the first photo-arms down, weight shifting back, slightly off-balance. Now notice the strong stance, forward drive and weight shift, and straight line from the wrist to the shoulder down to the hips and heels. Note too her facial expression went from "Oh, no!" to "Not today, pal!!" as her mindset shifted from one of helplessness to one of empowerment. Very, very well done.

This photo, taken during a women's self-defense seminar given by the Author, demonstrates the flow of technique from chin jab to eye rake. Note the drive from the hips and legs and the use of her left arm to aid in driving forward. "Helpless victim" my ass.

Upper Body Technique # 7: AXE HAND

The perfect marriage of forward pressure and body rotation.

Although it looks similar at first glance, this is NOT the stereotypical "karate chop." This motion is akin to swinging your arm as if it were a lead pipe. The focal point of the strike is the area below the pinkie finger to the mid-forearm, as shown in the above two pictures, respectively. Primary targets such as the throat and groin and secondary targets such as the sides and back of the neck are the most conducive to this strike.

MECHANICS
From the Non-Aggressive Ready Stance, rotate the hips away from the attacker slightly and then, using the hips and elbows in conjunction with one another, swing the arm down on a 45-degree angle as if trying to draw an "X" on the assailant from their shoulder to their opposite hip.

VARIATIONS
Although for purposes of this book the Axe Hand is trained out of the Non-Aggressive Ready Stance, it can be effectively applied from all 4 stances. In the Thinker/Jack Benny Stance, for example, the hand is already up and ready.

Also, the Axe Hand works wonderfully with Lower Body Technique#5-Foot/Toe Stomp. In this way, both the upper and lower body form a single cohesive unit. Think of it as a bad pro wrestling chest slap only for real.

The Axe Hand can also be applied effectively as a defense against a rear choke. By keeping the hips and elbows connected, as the defender swings his/her hand back towards the attacker's groin the entire body works together as one, causing a force of momentum very difficult to stop. Again, this works very well in tandem with an instep/toe foot stomp.

Upper Body Technique # 8: HAMMERFIST

The following photos were taken during a live workshop given by the Author. Note the position of her left foot, as it was used to deliver Lower Body Technique #5-Foot Stomp, just prior to her applying the Hammerfist.

MECHANICS
Delivered in almost exactly the same fashion as the Axe Hand, the Hammerfist uses the compact nature of the clenched fist to deliver a more "blunt force trauma" blow akin to that of a swinging hammer or wrecking ball. This makes it a particularly effective technique to smash an attacker's groin, again utilizing the swinging nature of the

arm, hip and elbow.

In fact, a workshop participant once stated she taught herself to remember the proper hand placement and use of the body to swing and deliver the strike by thinking of the Hammerfist as a "wrecking ball to wreck his balls." Nice! Ouch.

This "wrecking ball" principle can be seen in the sequence below. The defender rotates her hips into the strike and does not just flail her arm backward but uses her body as one unit.

Just after being grabbed. Note the weight shifting forward and shoulders shrugging upwards as the attacker grabs and pushes her forward to off-balance her.

A split second before the Hammerfist lands. Note the rotation of the body into the strike, not just the flailing of the arm. This is where your power comes from.

Against a side headlock position, the Hammerfist makes particularly useful tool against the only immediately available vital target. Note that the defender's right hand is grabbing the attacker around his waist to stabilize, and the victim's left foot will step into the attacker's force of pulling instead of trying to resist him while delivering the

Hammerfist. As the assailant doubles over, the defender will then continue to smash into his groin and eventually follow up to the eyes or throat to break free of the attacker's grip and get away or, if help is not available, continue his barrage in the most merciless, unforgiving way possible until the attacker no longer poses a threat.

"Self-defense is Nature's eldest law."

-John Dryden

Upper Body Technique # 9: "MONKEY SLAP"

Taken during a live workshop. Note the blurry nature of the hand on film, as it is relaxed and thereby able to transmit force and disperse energy effectively. Note, too, the defender's waist rotation and not merely swinging the arm.

The "Monkey Slap," when done properly, is a very potent self-defense weapon primarily due to the fact that the shape of the weapon used (i.e., the 5 digits of the hand cupping together as if to drink water from a stream) acts as an echo chamber that, when employed as a strike, causes the energy to disperse and hurt much more. The ideal targets for the Monkey Slap are the ears (either singular or simultaneous) to disrupt the assailant's equilibrium, or the groin.

Against a side headlock a monkey fist makes for a very effective weapon, as the energy disperses with a slap and the pain is magnified.

MECHANICS
When applying the Monkey Slap, the power does not come from the arm or the hand but rather the whole body. The rotation of the body is similar to that of the Evasion/Parry with the delivery of the Axe Hand and/or Hammerfist.

Please refer to the previous 2 photos once again. Practice this technique and all other techniques in this book from each of the 4 stances and from a variety of scenarios until you make them your own.

It is simply a matter of ingraining everyday motions into your muscle memory. If you've ever cupped your hand to drink water, you can do this technique perfectly. That's literally all there is to it.

Upper Body Technique # 10: ELBOW

Observe how the body twists on a center axis for greatest power generation.

Few techniques have the lethality or pure stopping power of a well-placed elbow. What makes this technique so vicious (i.e., effective), is the amount of force you generate in such a small distance. From your legs to your hips, to your waist, to your shoulders, to your elbow- all working as one unit and condensing all of that momentum into an area (the tip of your elbow) roughly the size of a half-dollar. Make no mistake-this is a fight-stopping technique, so it behooves you to learn to make it work for you.

MECHANICS
The elbow can either be performed with the lead or rear arm. See the following photos. When studying the

accompanying photo sequences, pay particular attention to the hip rotation of both elbow strikes, as this is where your power comes from.

Lead elbow:

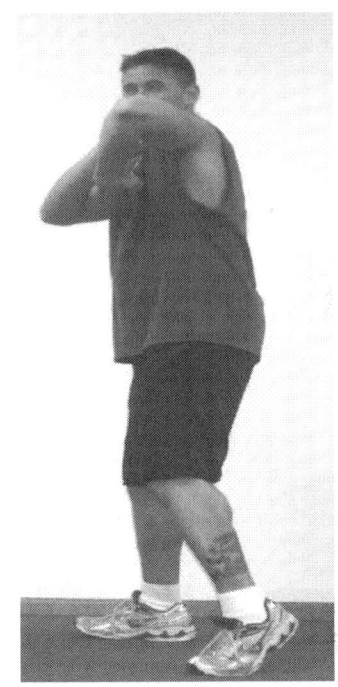

Note the foot and hip rotation as your body rotates on the center line.

Note the pivot on the ball of the lead foot as the elbow is delivered. As stated before, all of the force generated from the ground through the balls of the feet to the hips and trunk is distilled into the focal point of the strike-the bony protrusion of the elbow. It is not a "smack," it is a "scrape." The raking action of a well-placed elbow delivers all of the aforementioned force into an area the size of a half-dollar coin. Very potent, and potentially devastating. The same power generation can be seen in the following photo of an elbow delivered with the rear arm:

Rear elbow:

Again, notice foot pivot and hip rotation as strike is delivered.

In the following photo sequences pay attention to body movement in relation to the strikes-note the progression- first solo, then with the training tool.

The trajectory of an elbow can be:

Horizontal (as shown on the previous photos as well as next sequence on the following page)

Rotate on the axis from the tailbone to top of the head.

Always keep the opposite hand up in a guard position.

Vertical:

Diagonally Downward:

It all depends on what situation you find yourself in-don't make the mistake of "looking" to sink one of these in- practice all variations so you will be able to use them if you need to. One must be within trapping range to effectively execute the elbow strike properly. In order to do this, sink your weight slightly on both feet, rotate your waist into your strike and most importantly, do not stop once you've made contact. Think of slicing THROUGH something, rather than smacking something. This will create that ripping effect and inflict much more pain and cause much more damage to your attacker.

The following 2 sequences give you a feel for the different ways to apply the elbow strike. Note that these are just 2 of the numerous applications of this one strike. Elbows from a rear choke, bearhug from behind or headlock will be covered in the subsequent chapter on Extreme Situations and Close-Quarter tools. For the sake of learning the technique properly we are limiting the elbow technique in this manual to a frontal attack. You have to start somewhere and, like the adage goes, you must learn the form to become formless. As you begin to put your arsenal together, reference *Chapter 4: Lower Body Techniques* for notes on proper hip movement and footwork in this and all techniques.

Again, as with this or any other technique in this book, training with a partner is the only way to get the feel of flowing from technique to technique based on feeling and opportunity. Don't be hell-bent on delivering an elbow or a knee if the opportunity isn't there; stick within the confines of your vital targets and you will always have more than enough tools in your toolbox.

First the lead elbow application:

Note the short path of the elbow from the side of the body to the target.

Now the rear elbow application:

Note the same short path in conjunction with a tight rotation of the torso.

Some solid targets for the elbow would be:

- *Throat* (primarily horizontal elbow)
- *Bridge of nose* (horizontal or vertical depending on angle)
- *Cheekbone* (horizontal or vertical depending on angle)
- *Underside of Jaw* (primarily vertical elbow)
- *Solar plexus/Abdomen* (against an attack from the side or behind-see photos below):

Note the strong body unity and force generated...she's having none of this!

Note the rotation of the hips in conjunction with the driving action of the elbow as a force generator. The focal point (i.e., the bony protrusion) of the elbow is still the same. A slight variation can be performed using the elbow to defend against a tackle, as shown in the following sequence. Again, this is not a step-by-step guide *per se* (though the progression is valid) but rather a illustration of the concept of continuous attack.

"Hey man, I'm sorry I pissed you off...I don't want any troub-"

Bing!

"I told you I didn't want any trouble!"

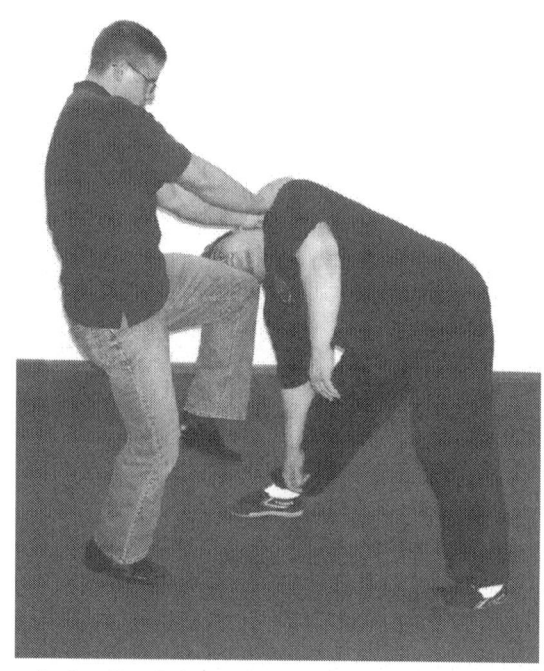

"There! Now where's the door? I'm getting the hell out of here..."

Upper Body Technique # 11: "HEISMAN TROPHY" WEB THROAT STRIKE

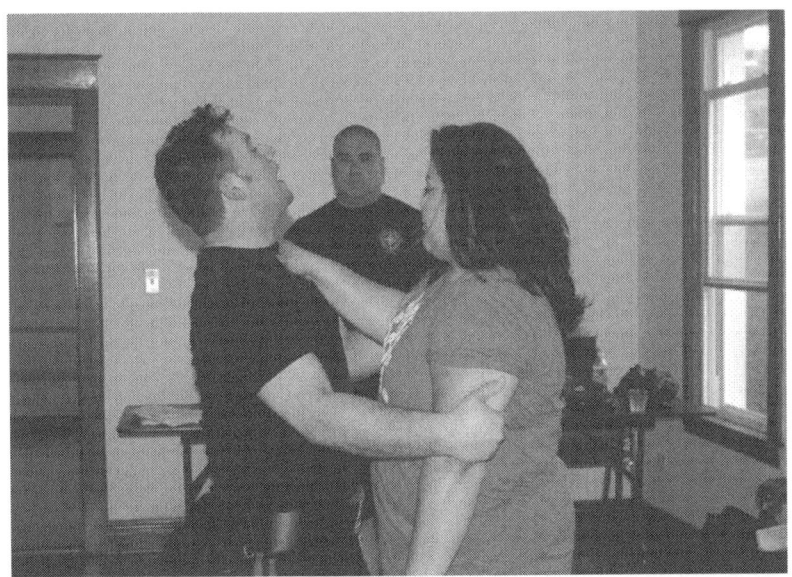

A first-time workshop participant applying the Web Throat/Heisman strike. The Author is not merely "playing along"- the shock to the throat causes one to literally concave. It is definitely an unpleasant experience to be on the receiving end of one of these and is a feeling that one must experience to truly appreciate.

The nickname for this technique comes from-you guessed it-college football's Heisman Trophy, on account of the posture of the trophy figure's right arm and the technique of a player running downfield with the ball "stiff-arming" opposing players en route to the end zone.

In the "Heisman Trophy" Strike, the focal point of the hand is the webbing between the thumb and the index finger. The ideal target to strike with this technique is the assailant's throat. The kinetic chain mentioned in the section on the Palm Heel (hand, wrist, elbow, shoulder, hip, legs) is employed again.

MECHANICS

To apply the lead hand strike, follow the body mechanics of the lead hand palm heel. The same goes for the rear hand web throat strike and the rear hand palm heel. In fact, think of this technique as applying the palm heel strike with a smaller stream of focus on a more vulnerable area. Think of it this way: the web throat strike wouldn't have the same effect if one hits an assailant in the face with it, as the surface area is much greater and requires a more blunt force trauma inducing surface, i.e., the palm heel. In the case of the throat, it is smaller, much more soft and extremely vulnerable to trauma, so the striking surface has to be more horizontal and penetrating.

The Heisman Trophy, collegiate football's highest honor. Note the extended arm and straight drive from the shoulder to the hand. Photo courtesy of the Heisman Trophy Trust.

Remember, too, the section of body mechanics on the Upper Body Technique #10-Elbow, as the torque of the hips and shooting out of forward pressure from the elbow as the webbing of the hand delivers the blow. Make no mistake, this is a potentially very damaging blow. Train on your partner's chest so that you can transfer the "stopping power" of this strike without hitting the actual target. All it takes is a slight change in aim to hit the throat, so don't practice on the throat until proper control is achieved.

Upper Body Technique # 12: HEADBUTT

There's a mistake in this picture...see if can you guess what it is.

    The headbutt is possibly the most lethal of the upper-body techniques and is ideally suited to be used against a larger assailant. You do NOT butt foreheads together. What you want to do is grasp around the opponent's neck, laying one hand in the palm of the other, and as you pull the opponent's face towards you, tuck your chin into your chest. The headbutt is simply slamming the opponent's face into the top of your head while pulling him in with your elbows and driving upward from the heels.

See photos below for proper hand and arm placement:

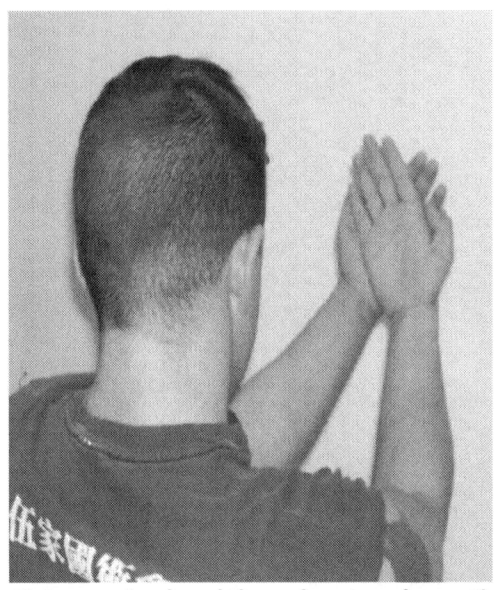

Picture a pin placed through your palms acting as a pivot point for clinching the sides of your attacker's neck while cradling the back of his head.

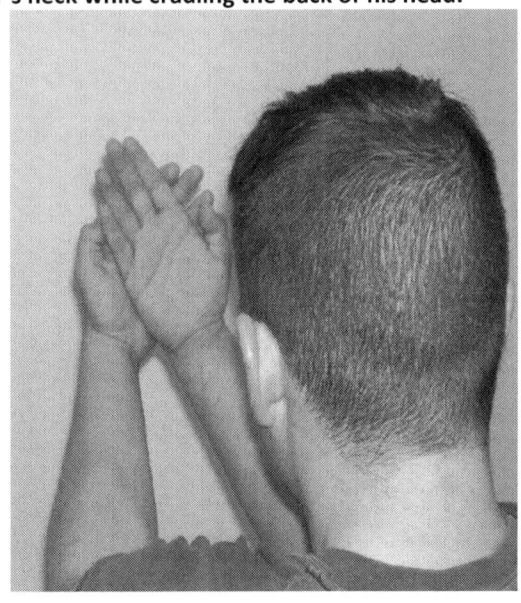

MECHANICS
To properly perform the headbutt, first latch onto your opponent's neck as shown in the above pictures and cinch your elbows in tight. This will put much pressure on the carotid arteries that run down the side of your neck, reducing blood flow to the brain and making it very uncomfortable for an attacker. If your opponent is under the influence and impervious to pain, the reduced blood flow to the brain elicits the same reaction as a choke. That is an important point to consider, as pain compliance is not always going to work if someone's tolerance is higher due to alcohol, drugs, adrenaline or just plain being a tough son of a bitch.

NOTE: You will find that it will be quite easy to move a body when in this position, as your elbows and hips will work together in conjunction with the footwork discussed in Chapter 4.

    After clinching, drop your center of gravity down. This will pull your attacker off base, even if they are stronger and especially if they are larger than you are. Drive with your hips, legs and gluteals (butt muscles), propel yourself upward off your heels (again, that kinetic chain of hip, knee and heel) as you pull into your center of gravity with your elbows. The middle of this "body sandwich" is your opponent's face. Be CAREFUL when practicing this. Have your partner tense his/her neck so as to avoid being on the receiving end of this for real. Also, don't dip your chin down-keep it straight and imagine your spine in one line, driving from the ground on an upward angle. Observe the following sequences:

First solo:

Drive up with the legs and hips while pulling down and in with the elbows.

Now with a partner:

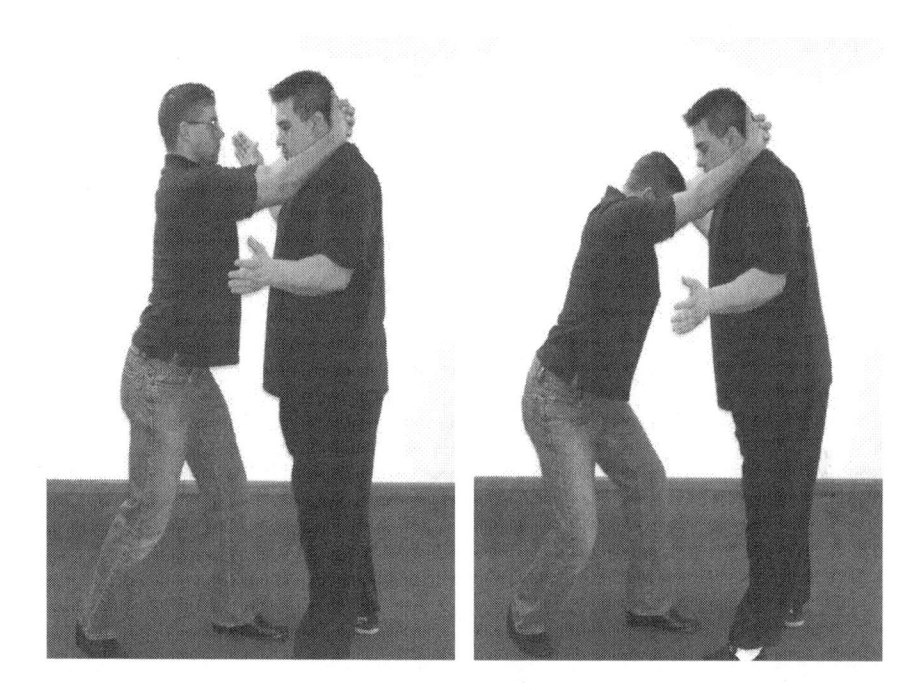

Sandwich his face between your clasped hands and the top of your head.

IMPORTANT

While we started this and all other technique progressions in this book from our Non-Aggressive Ready Stance, in reality most of your techniques will come into play in close proximity to your attacker by way of Upper Body Technique #2-Ice Breaker/Cow Catcher (please refer to the sequence on the following page). If you can intercept with an eyejab or a palm and then get away, that is optimal. If not, take your attacker out of commission as quickly as you can.

Upon sinking the headbutt, you will find that in most cases, the opponent will expose other targets. Therefore, following up with techniques to his vital targets in a logical manner might look something like this. Be sure to reference Chapter 4 for proper mechanics of the lower body. Refer to the following sequence as a sample of logical progression based on attack, target availability and opportunity.

Making my intent to avoid conflict known...

...which he obviously chooses to ignore so I employ the cow catcher as cover...

...followed by a clinch and headbutt...

...then a knee to the face...

...and finally an elbow to the temple for good measure!

Upper Body Technique # 13: BITE

The attacker isn't going to like what's coming up next.

    A note about this technique in particular: let me just say right off the bat that if you have to employ a bite, you need to recognize that the situation is very serious and the possibility for injury is very real. The bite is a LAST RESORT technique-for obvious reasons, we do not want someone else's blood in our mouths however if the choice is between that and not getting home to your family that night, that is a risk that I personally risk would be willing to take.

The two most necessary situations that would call for the use of a bite in that specific moment are as follows:

***Scenario 1:* the defender is choked from behind.** This is a *very* dangerous scenario-someone may be able to struggle with an attacker but if the bloodflow to the brain is cut off, the way it is in a rear naked choke, the defender will lose consciousness in less than 10 seconds. That is not one guy's opinion; that is medical fact.

Through proper training, as soon as the attacker begins to apply a rear choke the defender needs to drop his weight, and most importantly, tuck his chin to his chest. This will not feel good but I would much rather feel the pressure on my face than lose consciousness from a choke. As the chin tucks and the weight drops, the hands come up to the attacker's arms and the bite is sunk. As this happens the attacker will naturally try to pull away- it is up to you to, through your training and awareness, sense the opening for one of his primary targets and follow up with whatever attack suits the occasion.

***Scenario 2:* The defender is put in a side headlock**
Another common ambush street attack involves the side headlock. What is interesting to note is that it is human nature to resist force with equal and opposite force. Many times if an attacker applies a headlock they are looking to put the victim on the ground, especially in a male-female scenario. If your head is close to the attacker's side and no other targets are avaialble in that instant, turn into him, re-grab his waist and bite him hard. The bite to the soft area of the side of the body will be too painful and he will instincively not only let go but begin to push you away from him. Once again, it is at that moment you will need to have the proper training to follow up to the appropriate primary target and then get away to safety.

A final note about the bite: as I stated earlier if you

have to bite someone, things are bad. Therefore, if you need to apply the bite, really BITE them. If all you do is just nip once really quickly like a 15-pound pug/beagle mix, you will just piss them off. On the other hand, if you train yourself to hold the bite and continue to tear into them for a count of 3 to 5 seconds (in the "one-one thousand" counting style) you will make damn sure they get the message and become too preoccupied with how much they are in pain to focus on you. They will then try to get *you* off of *them,* allowing you to continue to one of their vital targets or get away. This requires a return to a primal, animalistic essence-one that we all have, no matter how "civilized" society becomes, and one that is ESSENTIAL for surviving an attack where a bite is warranted.

"If there's any guy crazy enough to attack me, I'm going to show him the end of the world -- close up. I'm going to let him see the kingdom come with his own eyes. I'm going to send him straight to the southern hemisphere and let the ashes of death rain all over him and the kangaroos and the wallabies."

— Haruki Murakami

CHAPTER 4
LOWER BODY TECHNIQUES

Lower Body Technique # 1:
ASTERISK FOOTWORK / EVASION

The first technique, much like the first Upper-Body technique, is not a "technique," per se but a method of transportation and positioning, from which you can assess the situation and act accordingly. In a proper Non-Aggressive Ready Stance as you'll recall, the feet are approximately 1 to 1.5 steps apart, with a slight angle of the rear foot to give added stability.
The major lower body movements can be generalized into 9 basic categories:

- Forward Shuffle/Advance
- Rear Shuffle/Retreat
- Sidestep Right
- Sidestep Left
- Forward Angle Left
- Forward Angle Right
- Backward Angle Left
- Backward Angle Right
- Quarter Turns- A major part of the Evasion/Parry Upper Body Technique #1; To perform a Quarter Turn, imagine your lead foot nailed down through the toe. Pivot on the ball of foot, keeping your hands up and weight even. Practice rotating 90 degrees to left and right from both a right and left lead until you are comfortable shifting to evade any attack whenever it calls for use of a quarter turn (i.e., deflecting and diffusing a strong oncoming force). Refer to the picture of the compass rose on the following page as a footwork "cheat sheet."

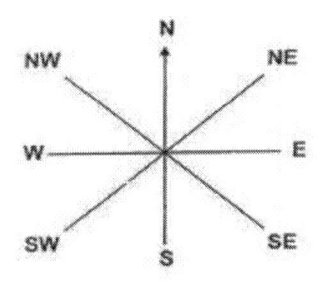

All of your necessary footwork patterns can be traced to this diagram of the compass.

Note: In all of the following pictures, I am in a left lead. For a right lead, all of the same rules stated herein apply. It takes a bit of practice to get comfortable with both sides, so never favor one over the other.

The Forward Shuffle used to advance in an attack, such as the eye-jab or palm heel, or an interception motion like the "cow-chaser." This is based on the Chinese art of Wing Chun (Ving Tsun) kung fu, and the footwork used in conjunction with the rapid-fire hand techniques prevalent in that system. It is no wonder that Wing Chun is so effective as a self-defense art.

MECHANICS
To perform the Forward Shuffle, simply take a small step with the front foot while simultaneously pushing off the rear foot. The rear foot should have a certain feel of springiness to it, yet at the same time feel a definite sense of being pulled along as the front foot advances. *NOTE: As with all footwork, there should be a light tension on the inner thighs, so as one leg advances or retreats, the other one is pulled in the same direction, almost like a bungee cord or rubber band is tied to both ankles. This will preserve your structure and help ground you as you employ any technique.* It will also serve to make any technique you use much more economical, as your body will be one

unit instead of a collection of unorganized parts. It may seem a bit foreign at first, but a little practice will convince you of its benefit. For further detail, refer to the following sequence of photos:

Keep light inward tension between the inner thighs to move as one unit.

Rear Shuffle / Retreat
This is an exact replica of the forward shuffle with one slight variation-can you guess what it is? Yep-this time you're moving backwards. In this case, it is the front foot

that pushes backward and the rear foot that takes a small step backward. The front foot has the feeling of being taken along for the ride, although there is no actual "dragging" in either case, as both feet are shifting on the balls, much like a boxing stance.

For further clarification, see the photo sequence below:

Again, just as with the Forward Shuffle keep the inward tension on the inner thighs to move the body as one unit, and hands up in a defensive position.

Sidestep Right

From a left-lead stance, the rear foot will step to the right first, followed by the left foot in the same direction. The manner of stepping and all other previous rules to the shuffle step apply here as well, i.e., keeping balanced on the center, not leaning, maintaining your structure and keeping a slight bounce in your step, not being "dead legged."

A Sidestep to the right-

Note how the tension on the thighs works laterally as well.

    At all times maintain the Non-Aggressive Ready Stance posture as described earlier. Think of that lead toe as the turret cannon on a tank; it points at your opponent- where your opponent goes, it goes. Sidetsepping will allow you to maintain structure at all times while either in assessment, offense or defense mode.

Sidestep Left

From a left-lead stance, the lead foot will step to the left first, followed by the rear foot in the same direction. The manner of stepping and all other previous rules to the shuffle step apply here as well, i.e., keeping balanced on the center, not leaning, maintaining your structure and keeping a slight bounce in your step, not being "dead legged."

A Sidestep to the left-

Always keep the weight on the balls of the feet for ease of movement.

An example of shuffle footwork and sidestepping in action can be seen in the following evasion sequences. Note that my hand positions sometimes differ from the prior photos- hey, it's a fight! It's an organic thing, one that is always changing, and one must continually adapt WITHOUT compromising structure or concept. My hand is always up in checking mode and my elbow is in-stick to the basics of the stance and make it work for you.

A sidestep shuffle to the left...

And one to the right...

Note that in both instances I was able to detect an attack and react accordingly. By evading successfully I am now able to exercise a variety of options: continue evading while attempting to verbally de-escalate the situation if this is a drunken buddy or family member who I know means no harm, get the hell out of there if the means are available, or if I NEED to, go for his vital areas (eyes, throat, balls) as well as his knees, shins or insteps as in this scenario they present themselves quite nicely for an oblique kick, as will be discussed later in this Chapter.

POINTS TO REMEMBER ON FOOTWORK & EVASION
- Keep your weight centered-do not lean in the direction you will move to. Think of the Irish dancers and how their bodies are always centered no matter where their feet go
- When moving, keep weight on the balls of the feet-do not keep feet flat on the floor
- Always remain aware of your foot placement-do not ever cross your feet-the intricate twisting moves you see on "Kung Fu Theatre" have no place here or anywhere in real life self defense as far as I'm concerned.
- Be aware of the relationship between your elbows and hips. As the elbows move, so do the hips. Keep the body rotating on the center axis when you employ the Upper Body Technique #1 Evasion/Parry, as seen in the following photo sequence. For clarification, re-visit Chapter 3.

Let us look at the the Evasion Footwork one more time, from both sides, within the context of Upper Body Technique #1-Evasion Parry. The footwork applies to every Upper Body Technique presented, this is just one example:

An attack from the defender's left side:

Don't swat his arm away; rotate and guide it past you while keeping your pressure forward and your body as one unit. Never let your arms cross your centerline, hence the rotation on the center axis.

An attack from the defender's right side:

Another view of moving your body as one unit. Again, don't cross center!

Lower Body Technique # 2: SHIN/KNEE OBLIQUE KICK (LEAD & REAR)

This technique is meant to be used when an opponent presents one foot in front of the other, giving you the knee or shin. Turn your front foot outward on a 45-degree angle as you lift your leg and step through and down, making contact with your heel, or if wearing shoes, the inner arch. Think of stepping "through" and "in," like propping a stick against a wall to snap it with your foot.

MECHANICS - Method A "Stomp" (Lead & Rear Leg)
From your Non-Aggressive Ready Stance, simply pick up your lead or rear foot (whichever is kicking) and stomp down onto the knee or shin of your attacker. Turn your hip out so that the sole of your foot lands squarely on the area you wish to smash. Again, think of propping a stick against a wall to break it by stomping into the center.

MECHANICS - Method B "Sweep" (best used with REAR leg). From your Non-Aggressive Ready Stance, shift your weight on your front foot, and suddenly sweep your rear foot up in a direct line to the opponents' shin. The point of contact is again the heel or if wearing shoes, the inner arch.

Note in both cases the hands are up and the elbows in. The hand and arm placement of the Non-Aggressive Ready Stance is constant so as to serve as both a quick defense and an opportunity for offense.

Method A (Stomp) Front:

As you lift the stomping knee, transfer the weight to the base leg. To keep balanced and for ease of transfer of power the knee should not raise past 90 degrees, lest you run the risk of being "jammed up."

Note that in the Stomp, the knee is lifted to the side first, then extended, propelling the heel and sole of foot towards the target. To accentuate and magnify the force generated, tuck the hips forward as you extend the knee. This will create a diagonally straight line between your heel all the way up to your torso.

Method A (Stomp) Side:

This kick, called a *chasse bas* ("Sha-say-*Bah*") in the French martial art of *Savate*, has its roots in back-alley street fighting and for good reason-if someone cannot stand, they cannot attack you!

Method B (Sweep): This motion would be akin to a pissed off manager sweeping sand on an umpire. See photo sequences below:

Method B (Sweep) Front:

Method B (Sweep) Side:

Note the kicking leg is nearly straight on the Sweep method.

Rest assured, as long as your weight is in the strike, you

do not need much effort to effect favorable results for either method. An example of the Method A (Stomp) shin/knee kick in a combative encounter. First the lead leg:

Note how upper body structure is maintained as the defender lands the kick.

Now the rear leg:

Note how the weight shifts to the base (left) leg as the stomp is employed.

Do not lean back when stomping but instead tuck the hips forward a bit, accentuating the power from your knee.

An example of the Method B (Sweep) shin/knee kick in a combative encounter:

The commitment of this kick is less since I am not stomping through.

As you can see the sweep doesn't land as high and my hip isn't as turned out. The sweep kick is more of a bang to the shin whereas the stomp kick is aiming to decimate the opponent's kneecap. Note in both cases the hands are up and in a defensive posture, as the body angles away from the strike, giving the attack that much more leverage. The power in the stomp variation comes from your weight being delivered into your opponent's kneecap. The power source of the sweeping variation comes from the hips and delivering the strike in a straight line from point A (the ground) to point B (the opponent's shin or kneecap). Ouch. Unlike the Stomp, there is no cocking of the knee because the mechanics and purpose of the strike are different. For the sweep, the hips are the prime mover as it is a quicker and less committed strike. Practice both equally.

Photo taken during a live workshop. A first-time participant applying a Method B Sweeping kick was shocked to feel how much power he generated with the hips sweeping the heel from point A (the floor) to point B (the assailant's shin). Thank God for the pads.

Lower Body Technique # 3: KNEE (LEAD & REAR)

Driving up and in from the hips = devastating amounts of force.

MECHANICS

Contrary to the movies, the knee is not an "up" technique although in cases like the groin it can be. Rather, an effective knee, such as the ones thrown by *muay thai* boxers, raises until the thigh is parallel to the floor, then the hips are thrust forward, driving the knee inwards. The hands will clinch around the attacker's neck, elbows in to keep control. Slightly lean back to accentuate the thrust of the hips. Refer to the following photo sequences:

Lead knee (front)

Note how the knee raises until the thigh is parallel then penetrates forward.

Notice how the elbows are in to aid not only in protecting the body from being bear-hugged but also in cinching the neck and/or pulling the assailant into the knee by using the muscles of the back to pull from the elbows, much the same as an abbreviated rowing motion.

Lead knee (side)

The hips play an integral role in the lead knee for lack of drive from the legs.

Rear knee (front)

The rear knee is a more powerful strike but don't get sloppy and overcommit!

Rear knee (side)

Note how the thigh raises until parallel and then thrusts forward from the hips as the arms pull the attacker into the strike.

An example of a front knee used in a combative encounter:

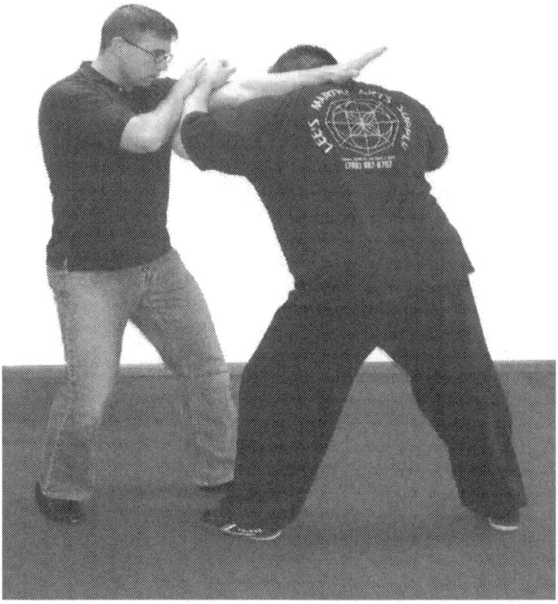

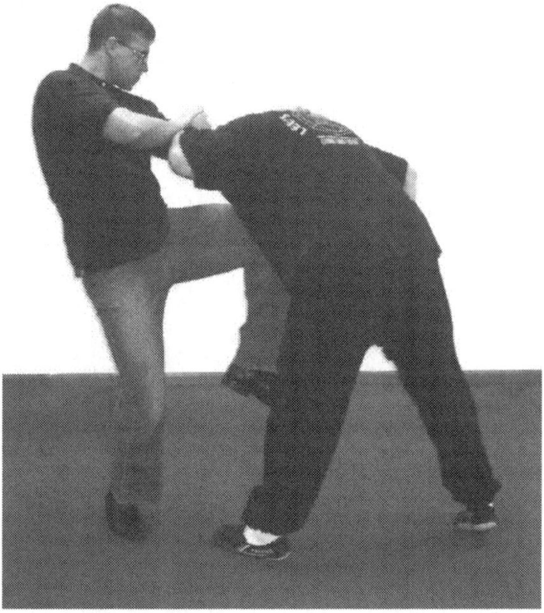

An example of the rear knee executed in a combative encounter:

Observe if you will that in both instances (lead and rear knee) that upper body techniques were used to "bridge the gap" from the Non-Aggressive Ready Stance to the execution of the knee strike. A knee is a close-range technique and is best employed when one is in *trapping* (headbutt, knee, elbow and eye rake) range, as dictated in Chapter 2.

The front knee will require a shuffle step (we will cover the "pendulum swing" footwork later in this Chapter) to gather the necessary momentum, whereas the rear knee is already positioned to deal an effective blow. Either way, the knee is a potent technique that is capable of inflicting massive damage. This is in no small part due to the force generated by the hips, as the waist is the strongest junction on the body. Anyone who doubts this need only ask a practitioner of Brazilian *jujutsu,* an art of which leverage of the hips plays a pivotal role.

Yes, the ladies always relish the idea of kneeing a guy in the plums.

A workshop participant ready to drive that knee in to the attacker. What is amusing is that less than a half an hour prior to this photo being taken she was a wallflower-now she's kicking ass and loving every second of it.

"I don't believe in fighting...I believe in beatings. Either me on you, or you on me. If you are in an actual fight then that means something went wrong with the technique."
- Anonymous

Lower Body Technique # 4: CLOSE-QUARTERS SHIN/FOOT SCRAPE

This technique can be employed any time one is in trapping range-particularly if one is in a position where your chest and the assailant's are facing the same direction (i.e., he is to your side).

MECHANICS
Simply place the heel or outer arch on the opponent's shin, just below the knee. Shift all of your weight to your attacking foot as you ride the shin down all the way to the instep, where you deposit all of your weight through your heel to the toe or instep. Think of having a 6-inch spike in your heel and you want to nail your attacker's foot to the floor and crush his bones like you are smashing a soda pop can on the ground. Drive all of your weight down through your heel into the ground This last stomping action will lead us into Lower Body Technique #5 – the most important facet of this technique (that is, technique #4) however, is the scraping action from the knee downward).

Come back to this technique after you learn Techniques 5 and 6. You will find that as you practice this technique more and more, this is a perfect time to begin with a knee kick (Technique #6), ride the shin bone down, scraping the nerves, and finishing with a heel stomp to the metatarsal bones of the foot and/or the toes (Technique #5). Of course, not every situation will beget the use of all of the techniques. It all depends on wherever you find yourself in relation to the attacker. Remember, situation begets target; target begets technique-not the other way around.

Observe the photo sequence on the following page:

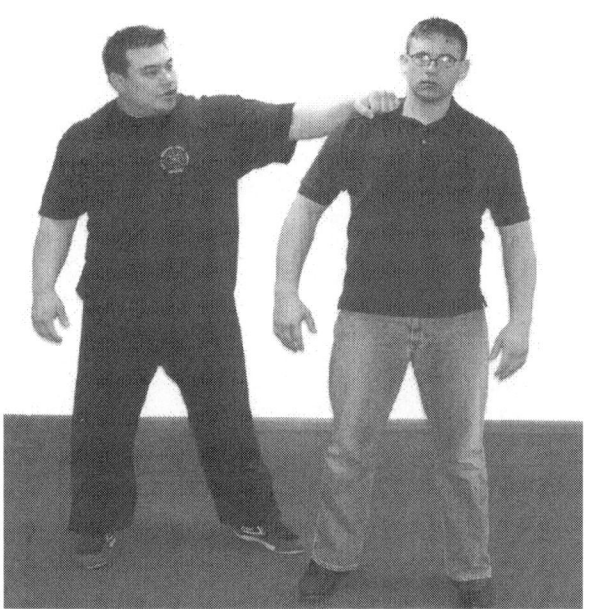

"I wonder what I should get for dinner-what the!!"

"I think I'll pin the arm, scrape down the shin and drive my heel through his foot like I have a spike for a foot!"

"Hmmm..that Axe Hand would fit nicely in his throat! Hey, if it's there..."

    This will not feel good. Have you ever woken up in the middle of the night to use the bathroom, and banged your shin on a nightstand or edge of a bed? Magnify that times ten and you get an idea of how potent this scraping action is. Observe too that in this scenario, the position of the Defender's right hand can be used to deliver the Upper Body Technique #7 - Axe Hand once the shin scrape is completed as one option of many. Hey, if it's open, why not? Let us take a page out of the late Count Dante's book as discussed in Chapter 1: A fight is almost always not won with only one technique; therefore we must train ourselves to respond in an overwhelming fashion to the vital targets of our assailant. Since we do not know what situation we will find ourselves in, stick to the objective of destroying the vital targets and you will never want for something to be open to you. Just remember to keep going until the threat is neutralized or you can remove yourself from the situation.

Lower Body Technique # 5: FOOT/TOE STOMP

This one can be done in conjunction with Lower Body Technique #4-Close Quarters Shin/Foot Scrape, or on its own any time the target presents. Ladies, wearing heels does have its advantage in this regard and men, wearing boots won't work against you in this case!
This is best used when an assailant is in your personal space or has grabbed you, as the opportunity to employ other techniques better suited to interception or longer range is limited. A major advantage to using the foot/toe stomp is the fact that the assailant's attention is on your "high line" (head and shoulders). He will not be concerned with nor will he be looking at your "low line" (legs, knees, feet). Practice this technique slowly at first, and then faster, all while not looking at his feet. Let your peripheral vision and sensory awareness of his body based on the energy (pressure) he gives you through the touch of his grab or his invasion of your personal space pick up where his feet are.

MECHANICS

Pick up your foot as if you are pulling your shoe out of mud. Do not raise your knee high at all. Think of sneaking up on a cockroach; if you raise your knee too high, it senses your movement. Simply pick up your foot, and step downward while dropping all of the weight into your heel. This minimal motion will not be sensed by a rise in your shoulders the way a knee raise-type action will. Deposit all of your weight through your heel, into your assailant's instep or toe and into the floor.

If someone grabs your shirt, step on his foot. Create space to either remove yourself from the situation and get the hell out of there, or if need be, claw his face and eyes, rip at his throat and knee or grab his balls. If you react to an attack like a cute little kitty-kat who just got doused with water, your odds of getting away just went up dramatically. Refer to the following sequence:

Knowing the attacker is becoming belligerent and aggressive, the defender assumes a Thinker/Jack Benny stance.

Once the attacker encroaches into the defender's personal space, it's game-on!

Note how the defender grabs the attacker as he steps down on his instep, setting up for a rapid counter-offensive. This motion is so slight and quick the attacker has little if any time to react.

Depositing the full body weight into the attacker's instep. From here the defender's right hand will shoot towards the eyes, throat or the balls (and ideally, a combination of all 3).

A logical progression from this technique can be seen in the following sequence. Again, this is not a step by step guide *per se*, but a logical progression based on target availability. See the following:

The defender's hands instinctively come up in that flinch response everyone has when responding to stress. This creates a "bridge" between the attacker and her to read the attacker's pressure through her arms touching his.

Beginning to employ the counter-offensive. The attacker obviously has no idea what's coming next-or how much he isn't going to like what's in store for him.

Note how the defender re-grabs the attacker to control him...

Notice too how she went from the Foot Stomp right to the Chin Jab-from low line to high line-nice touch.

From the Chin Jab down to the Eye Rake...

...and driving it home with a Rear Knee Strike to the balls.

Note how the attacker is now helpless and completely out of his element, i.e., from attack to off balance and at the mercy of the "victim."

An interesting point to mention is that the Eyes and Groin are what is referred to as "brother-sister targets," meaning attacking one will almost always open up the other. Something to keep in mind: if someone pokes me in the eyes, what happens? I bring my hands to my face and instinctively lean backwards exposing my groin. On the other hand, if I am hit in the groin, what happens? I clutch my groin and pike my hips back and butt out, leaning forward exposing my face which then begets the eyes and throat as targets.

Through proper training, scenario drills, technique repetition, body position familiarity etc. the right tool will come out at the right moment at the right time. Remember, learning this system is a skill set, and as the saying goes, "repetition is the mother of skill." Remember too, that just like any other skill set, this System must be practiced and practiced correctly for as another wise saying goes, "practice does *not* make perfect; only perfect practice makes perfect." Either way-practice!

Lower Body Technique # 6: SIDE KNEE KICK

"You want some? You got it! I'm gonna snap your knee like a matchstick."

The side knee kick is a potent close-range weapon when an attacker is to your side. Again, think of propping a stick against the wall to break it-only in this case, the "stick" is the knee of your attacker.

MECHANICS
As your attacker approaches you and/or grabs you, simply lift up your leg and step down and in forcefully against his knee. Your weight should travel in an unbroken line from your heel (or arch if wearing shoes) to his knee. Think of this as an inverted Stomp Kick, hinging from the hip while turning your knee inward instead of outward. The Stomp Kick is used for a frontal attack while the Side Knee Kick is used, well, obviously, for attacks from your side but the general principles and concept remains the same. Refer to the following photo sequence:

As the attacker lunges in, the defender needs to utilize the side shift of Lower Body Technique #1: Asterisk Footwork/Evasion, to shift his weight and "base out" so as not to be pushed over.

Much like Lower Body Technique #2A - Stomp Kick, the knee is raised as the weight is shifted, and shot out like a piston into either the front or side of his knee.

This flows nicely into the Close Quarters Shin/Foot Scrape (Lower Body Technique #4), as seen below:

From here the defender can follow up as quickly and forcefully as possible to any open targets and get the hell away.

Note: techniques # 5 and 6 work best when one is in a situation where the distance between you and your assailant is so small that many other techniques cannot be effectively used. In other words, lunging for someone's instep is not a good idea; stomping on their toe or scraping their shin and then following up with an eye rake or groin grab when they grab a hold of you and invade your comfort zone or personal space is. Training in a variety of scenarios and conditions is the only way to get that sense of flow and familiarity.

> Acknowledgement: I would like to sincerely thank my training partners Ron Lewis and Melissa Wilder for demonstrating the preceding techniques. Melissa is a 3rd degree black belt in the Combat Hand Integration (CHI) Eclectic Martial Art Systems, as well as a 2nd degree black belt in Shidokan full-contact karate. Born and raised in the Bronzeville section of Chicago's south side, Ron is a Vietnam combat veteran of the elite 101st Airborne Division. As a result of their respective experience, both of their "bullshit meters" are finely tuned regarding matters of practicality and realism as it pertains to self-defense and both have ample experiences to share with us in class. On a personal note, two more attentive and dedicated training partners and nicer people I could not hope to meet.
> Thank you both so much.

> *"I don't call it violence when it's self-defense, I call it intelligence."*
> -Malcolm X

Lower Body Technique # 7: SHUFFLE KICK (FRONT & ROUND)

A "pot-shot" to the balls...

...or to the inside of the knee.

These two techniques will require a remedial level of speed and footwork and, dare I say, finesse. They are to be used as "stun and run" techniques as they generally speaking lack the stopping power of many of the other techniques to effectively halt an attacker in his tracks. What these techniques will do is open a split-second window of opportunity for you to get where your game is-trapping range. You may notice that I have listed these two techniques (front and round) as one technique when they are two different kicks. This is because even though the mechanics of the kicks themselves are slightly different the concept remains the same and that's really what we're all about-simplifying techniques into concepts that can be applied by whatever situation we are thrust into.

The most opportune time to use a shuffle kick is when it has been declared, either verbally or nonverbally, that you are in a fight. Now that you know you're in "the shit", you need to assess the situation and react (or act, which would be more fitting to our line of strategy) accordingly. Shuffle kicks allow us to assess, attack, and retreat within a very small window of time. This is accomplished by using what is known as a "pendulum swing" of the feet, as seen in the following sequence. Note the hands stay up in a defensive posture and do not flail out to the side to aid in balance. This is what is known in martial arts and boxing circles as "telegraphing," or giving off clues visa body mechanics that a strike is coming. Notice howthe shoulders stay level, the hands do not move and the weight is shifted seamlessly from the lead to the rear foot as the lead foot makes a straight line from ground to groin.

Please refer to the following sequence for a different perspective on this same technique. Pay particular attention to the body mechanics of this strike.

A shuffle kick using pendulum footwork – front angle:

Note that the weight shift replaces the need to cock the front knee.

A shuffle kick using pendulum footwork- side angle:

Note that the weight stays in a straight line from the floor as the feet switch.

The pendulum swing is nothing more than a re-positioning of the feet, with an exaggerated shuffle forward and backwards step. The real "money maker" of this kick is the hips. The hip loads as the rear foot slides up and then and then pops forward as the weight sinks on the rear leg. For the front kick, as you shuffle forward, do not chamber your knee and snap the kick out. To do so robs the kick of much of its power by relying on the strength of the knee joint instead of the tremendous thrusting power of the hips. In order to effectively channel this power source, as you shuffle forward, raise your leg up naturally. You will find a certain degree of bend in the knee to begin with. Now, thrust your hips up and forward as you make contact with the instep (shoelace area) of your foot to your attacker's groin area – think "up" & "in!" Observe the following sequence and pay attention to the hands and footwork:

"Okay, he's big, looks pissed and I can't talk my way out of this sh*t...now what?"

"His hands are up-there's no doubt anymore. I'm going for the balls!"

BING!

My hands are always up in a defensive posture yet ready to launch any of my Upper Body techniques from Chapter 3, and my rear leg is slightly bent to support my weight as I drive with my hip.

For the shuffle round kick, the mechanics remain the same but the hip delivering the kick turns slightly over, creating a 45-degree upward-angled attack. This short, upward motion is aimed at the groin area but the circumstances for their respective uses are quite different. In this scenario, my assailant has made it known to me that we are in a fight. Since I have no choice, and I am too far away to get into trapping range and poke his eyes or grab his balls, I have to use my evasion footwork and look to "pot shot" him so I can get away. In fact, in any self-defense scenario I would prefer not to even have to get to trapping range, as that carries with it an increased likelihood that I can be injured as well.

"Okay, he's big, looks pissed and I can't talk my way out of this sh*t...now what?"

"Not squared up, I can't get to the jewels...that knee looks a bit exposed, though. So be it!"

The front kick is used when the attacker is squared up to you (shoulders forward, giving you a clear shot at the groin). Obviously, hitting the groin when the opponent is in a combative or fighting stance cannot be done in an effective manner using the front kick, so in this instance the round kick is used. In this instance, my opponent has quite a reach advantage and the angle of his knee is such that hitting the groin isn't as clear at that moment as I'd like. No problem, I just went to the knee instead. From here I will follow up with attacks to the eyes, throat or groin and look to take him out of commission or, if that did the trick, high-tail my ass out of there. Note that the point of contact to the assailant's knee with the round kick is the same as the front kick to the groin, i.e., the instep/shoelace area.

Taken during a live workshop. Note the thrust of the hips and the tucking in of the buttocks to drive the kick home. This is different from the standard martial arts kick which relies heavily on snap, as in this case we want to drive up and in, smashing the testes against the pubic bone...just lovely.

CHAPTER 5
EXTREME SITUATIONS & WEAPONS TRAINING

Extreme Situations

This section is quite short, and intentionally so. Allow me to share a personal anecdote that explains why: Once while teaching a women's self-defense workshop I had a participant who I could tell very early on would be a bit of a challenge to put it mildly. She wanted to address so many different scenarios almost right after we began each new technique. I could tell that, although being the type that after about an hour could probably make Jesus himself want to duck out to the local pub for a shot and a beer, her heart was in the right place. I finally had to explain to her and the class that addressing car-jackings, plane takeovers, hostage situations and the like was completely useless if the basics of what I am teaching in this class aren't grasped. Like the old adage goes, "How do you fight three people? The same way you fight one."

I often ask my classes and workshops, after we have been drilling the techniques in this book for a while,
"What would you do if you are grabbed from behind on the bike path?" "How about if you are carjacked?" "How would you react if you are grabbed walking to your car in a dark parking lot at night with an armful of groceries?" and so on. It is interesting to note that they almost always get the deer-in-the-headlights look as they begin processing the specifics of each scenario. The reason for their blank gazes stems from the fact that they are letting the scenario dictate their game plan when in reality the game plan is the one thing that should NEVER waiver. The point I am making is that any situation when you are attacked is an "extreme" one. In order to convey the information in the preceding chapters a clean slate, perfect scenario was needed, which is why the scenarios presented via photographs were always

one-on-one in a spacious studio with no gravel, parking blocks or curbstones anywhere. This is how one must learn the techniques, *but it is almost always never how one must apply them should they need to.*

Chapter 6 will detail the training progression we use for any technique or skill set but insofar as "extreme situations" are concerned, keep this in mind: if you can conceive any possible scenario in your head, so can someone else and it's already been a scenario in which someone was attacked, raped and possibly killed before. The greatest training tool you could ever ask for is right between your ears. Simply picture different scenarios you may find yourself in, and then train in them. By adhering to our approach (i.e., situation dictates target, target dictates technique) and going for the vital targets (eyes, throat and balls) you will never want for scenarios to train. Inside, outside, grass, gravel parking lots, if you can think of it, train in it.

Practice coming out of your car or going to your car. Practice in a closet or doorway. Practice in different shoes and clothes. Practice outside when it is cold and windy and drizzly or hot, foggy and muggy. Practice in the blinding light of the sun and in the blackness of a moonless night. Since it is imperative that both men and women get a feel for being on the ground, practice being taken to the ground, either by headlock, tackle or in women's cases a rapist either straddling them or on top of them. The more scenarios you are familiar with the more you can see that the targets are still there, waiting to be hit. That is the key to training, seeking and finding commonalities among several different scenarios. The next Chapter will discuss how this can be done safely and in a thorough, logical and progressive way.

Weapons Training

This section is also very short, and for good reason. Oftentimes when discussing all things self-defense and personal protection related, one of the most commonly asked questions involves, "how do you deal with a weapon?" or "what do you do if the attacker has a weapon?" My response is always that working with weapons adds an entirely new dimension to one's training but the concepts are the same as empty handed fighting. Unfortunately, this aspect of training is also one of the biggest offenders in promoting both completely unrealistic and overly complex reactions to weapons attacks (such as some martial arts systems that seriously teach students to kick a knife out of the hand of an attacker and continue the motion with another spinning kick – seriously?!) as well as the "paralysis by analysis" addressed earlier, brought on by practicing totally different responses to specific attacks.

Once again, in line with our philosophy of simplification and drawing parallels and commonalities between concept and technique, the *Walking Weapon Self Protection Skills System* uses a very simple, direct and efficient method of dealing with weapon attacks which we call "De-Fanging the Snake." This training method is taken from several Filipino stick and knife arts and is simply this: the attacker is the snake; his weapon is the fang. By hitting the hand with the weapon, he drops it...you have just de-fanged the snake. In any scenario, our primary response to any weapon attack should always be to attack the hand with the weapon in it, de-fanging the snake. In training, we will often use padded sticks and rubber knives to "spar" as we move around, simply trying to hit the opponent's hand with the weapon. This also develops quick reflexes, coordination, timing, increased reaction time and footwork. Now you may be reading this thinking to yourself, *"well that's just swell, but when am I going to carry a stick or knife with me?!"* Let me ask you this:

Do you carry keys?
Do you read a magazine or newspaper on the train or the bus?
Do you carry a water bottle?
A jacket?
A purse?
A cell phone?
Do you wear a belt?
Do you carry spare change?

Anything can become a "weapon of opportunity" in the right hands. Spare change flung into an attacker's eyes, a belt buckle swung into an attacker's hand or face, a spray of water in the eyes, a rolled up magazine or keys swung to the hand of an attacker's weapon, his eyes, throat or groin, a dog leash, a pool cue, an ashtray and so on…all of these are weapons, and all of them can be used to attack an assailant's vital targets and/or "de-fang the snake."

Try this drill: roll up two magazines and rubber band or duct tape them nice and tight. No go to an open space and have your training partner try and hit you with one. Instead of trying to block and disarm each specific attack like most shopping mall martial arts schools show you (which I can almost guarantee will get you killed) simply try and hit the hand holding the magazine. Not only is it a whole lot simpler, your footwork will improve considerably, your awareness will be sharpened and your mindset will shift from a reactive one to a proactive one. Have at it.

CHAPTER 6
TRAINING PROGRESSION & RECOMMENDED EQUIPMENT

Training Progression

There have been many techniques, principles and concepts covered in this book. Now comes the part of functionalizing these techniques. There are 4 stages of any technique:

First, you **LEARN** the technique. This is done in a controlled environment, with little or no variation to familiarize you with the specifics of the technique itself.

Second, you **PRACTICE** the technique. This involves repetition after repetition, still in a controlled environment, to ingrain the motions into your subconscious and muscle memory.

Third, you **MASTER** the technique. Mastering a technique does not mean you can apply it in combat; it simply means you know how to do the technique, correctly, very well.

Once someone has mastered a technique, they must learn how to apply it in a non-cooperative situation (training, drills, sparring, and hopefully should the need arise, real-life combat). This process is known as the **FUNCTIONALIZATION** of the technique. Quite frankly, all three previous stages, while necessary to get you to step 4, don't mean shit if step 4 isn't achieved.

So, take any technique from this book and begin applying the following training formula:

Solo Training: Train the technique without an opponent.
- Technique only
- Progressive contact and speed

- Imagined Scenario (with dialogue, verbal diffusion, etc.)

Partner Training: Now add someone to practice on.
- Technique only
- Progressive contact and speed
- Scenario (with role play and dialogue, verbal diffusion, etc.)

Multiple Partners: Increase the amount of people you train with
- Technique only
- Progressive contact and speed
- Scenario (with role play and dialogue, verbal diffusion, etc.)

Once that stage of training is reached, begin to add in some Situational Awareness Drills. Train in different environments to get a feel for different situations you may find yourself in where you may need to resort to one of these techniques. The sky is the limit on this one. Any place you may find yourself in during the course of a day is fair game for training. Some tips on variation in training environment:
- Indoors –day and night to get lighting changes
- Outdoors-day and night to get lighting and weather changes
- Strobe light
- Music playing loudly – this creates sensory overload
- "White noise" – this unpleasant sound instantly takes you out of your comfort zone

You get the idea. You are only limited by your imagination-but you have to start somewhere. This is why all of the techniques in the book are shown in a very one-dimensional way. A real fight is scrappy, sloppy and completely unpredictable. If you train either in this picture-perfect scenario way or swing too far to the opposite end of the spectrum right off the bat, i.e., full on scenario training, you will gain next to nothing. Training must be progressive in every sense if it is to be successful and effective.

The fact remains that no matter how intense training is, it is just that: training. One thing that is above question, however, is the reality that you will respond in direct proportion to how you train. If you train in the above manner, both progressively and realistically, your chances of being able to successfully apply any of this stuff increase. If you do not, your chances go the wrong way.

As I stated in the first Chapter, proper training just gives you slightly better odds and, in all reality, that's about as good a position as you can hope for should the need to apply this stuff ever surface. That is not pessimism; that is just reality. All you can hope to do is give yourself as good a chance as you can to get home in one piece. One may read this and take this viewpoint as negativity; I disagree. There is a sense of liberation and freedom in not lying to oneself.

Please approach your training in this vein.

"After initial contact, all plans go to hell."
-General George S. Patton

Recommended Equipment

In order to maximize your training, contact has to be made. The following is a short list of equipment I have found to be most useful and applicable in training.

A full-body suit such as those manufactured by Predator Armour (the best out there) is best for allowing full power shots to the vital areas but they run upwards of $2,500 or so, putting them well out of reach for most people. No worries, there are still several budget friendly options that provide all manner of realistic training.

Mouthpiece: First and foremost, a solid mouthpiece will ensure you don't bite your tongue, chip your teeth or get concussed while practicing techniques such as the chin jab.

Mitts: Focus pads/mitts such as those used by boxers are necessities for gaining the feeling of hitting a real target at full power.

Body Shields/Chest Protectors: These are necessary for landing full power shots to the solar plexus such as rear elbows and knees.

Shin Guards: Catcher's gear or solid heavy-duty leather kickboxing shin pads like those made by Fairtex work well for absorbing full power shots to the shin.

Motorcycle Helmet: Without a doubt the only type of face protection I have found to be able to withstand elbows, knees, headbutts, and any other strike. A bit pricey, but worth its weight in gold for realism-they are made for heavy impact, after all!

MMA Gloves: It's always good to have a pair of MMA training gloves handy. You never know when a hand will hit an elbow or knee in training...

Groin Protector/"Diaper:" Boxers use these while training and sparring. They resemble an oversized diaper and cover the groin and hips. Obviously they will not provide adequate protection to the groin – hold a focus mitt out in front of you and let your partner hit it with the visual reference point of your body instead.

Dummy knife, stick, gun, etc: Great for practicing defenses against muggings, robberies, rape scenarios and the knife and sticks are great for drills such as De-Fanging the Snake.

Goggles (Racquetball or Competitive Swimming style): These allow an "attacker" to be eye raked and gouged as the defender feels their face, cheeks, nose, etc., gaining valuable tactile experience by feeling the eyebrows, cheekbones, etc.

Any other equipment that suits the drill: Get creative on this one. Spare change, water bottles, dog leashes, shoes, belts, rolled up magazines, keys, you name it. Make it your own. You know you; you know what you carry with you. Train with it!

> *"Train with what you have, not with what you wish you have."*
> *-Anonymous*

CHAPTER 7
RECOMMENDED READING & "BRAIN TRAINING"

Building your Success Library:
Recommended Reading

World *shuaijiao* kung fu champion, national collegiate wrestling champion and internet entrepreneur/business coach Matt Furey hit the nail right on the head when he once stated that in order to be a success at anything, you have to amass and continually expand a personal library about whatever subject you wish to be a success in. This type of "brain training" and mental skill development is no different than anything else; you need to constantly fill your mind with information that will make you better than you are now. It is for this reason that I have included this section. Listed below are the books I have found most valuable thus far. Keep in mind that this list is always growing, just as we all should be as practitioners of the self-defense and combat arts, however, this will give you a solid foundation on which to build your mental training. Always remember that no successful person's library is ever complete, but no person ever became successful without one, either.

The Gift of Fear- **Gavin de Becker**
If there is one book for the layman and martial artist alike to read I would recommend this one. It details the root of the emotion of fear and how true fear exists to serve us. Fear is like a fire; it can either cook your food and keep you warm or it can kill you. De Becker, through several examples, illustrates how to distinguish and cultivate true fear and how to make it serve you.

On Killing: The Psychological Cost of Learning to Kill in War and Society- **Lt. Col. Dave Grossman**
Lt. Col. Grossman, a former U.S. Army Ranger and West Point graduate, details the process by which humans are

desensitized to kill and the resulting effect this process has on society. A fascinating look at the act of violence from a psychological point of view as well as its long-lasting effects and implications.

Meditations on Violence: A Comparison of Martial Arts Training and Real-World Violence- **Rory Miller**
This book should be required reading for anyone involved in the martial arts, as it addresses the main issue/problem with martial arts training as it relates to self-defense and personal protection. Miller also has other books out there; read them all. Fantastic material.

Tao of Jeet Kune Do- **Bruce Lee**
In his own words, Bruce Lee's thought process and blueprint for his evolution in martial arts. The technique sections of this book may not be all that useful for the non-martial artist, however, as a philosopher Lee's words on fighting, combat and the nature of self-protection ring just as true to the martial artist as they do to the general public.

Look Beyond the Pointing Finger: *The Combat Philosophy of Wong Shun Leung*- **David Peterson**
Peterson, a direct student and certified instructor under Grandmaster Wong Shun Leung, legendary bare-knuckle challenge match fighter of the Wing Chun system, presents his master's personal philosophy, mindset and approach to both martial arts and fighting for self-preservation. The concepts contained in this book form the bedrock for the *Walking Weapon Self Protection Skills System.* Wong always stressed the need to make whatever art you train work for you, not the other way around. This book gives you insights into his deep level of understanding of the true nature of combat.

***The Lazy Man's Guide to Enlightenment*- Thaddeus Golas**
The first sentence of the first chapter says really everything you need to know, *"We are equal beings and the Universe is our relations with each other."* A tiny little book and a simple read but one that needs to be read over and over in order to grasp the depth of what is being said. For students of the combat arts it helps to distill the idea of a calm and clear mentality without coming right out and saying so. Just as reading the Cliffs Notes version of *Crime and Punishment* won't give you the subtleties and nuances of the original writings, reading books specifically geared towards one topic or another, while valuable in one sense, will rob you of the thought process used to come to the same conclusions and, in turn, grow. Approach this book in the same way; read it and let it seep in. Sooner or later you'll get it and when you do the lessons contained in this book will be that much more entrenched in your mind.

"BRAIN TRAINING"

The cloistered monks living within the monasteries of the world are taught to "pray without ceasing." This doesn't mean they have to sit and recite the Lord's Prayer or some Buddhist sutra all day – if that's all they did then while they were busy getting in tune with the source of all creation, people would come and take all their shit away. What "praying without ceasing" really means is to let every act be a prayer in and of itself to God by doing the best one can do in whatever one is doing. Thus, you offer up the best of who you are to God. Brain training for self-defense is the same way. You just don't turn something like this off, nor do you punch out like a time-clock when training time is over. While it's a no-brainer that your body needs rest and recovery to repair itself, you can still train your mind constantly. This too doesn't mean that every waking moment is spent racked in contemplation of fighting, self-defense, techniques or scenario drills. What it means is to allow concepts such as instinct, awareness, and self-preservation seep into your subconscious to the point where they become ingrained in your mindset and as a result, certain habits become second nature.

Train yourself to immediately identify exits and means of egress in every building you walk into. Hone your observation skills while you are driving, walking or interacting with people. Don't ever "eyeball" anyone but make silent notes to yourself as to who is around and what methods can be used should you need to dispatch one of them quickly. For example, if I am around someone who is taller or bigger than myself, in a split second I size them up as to which targets I would go for first should I need to go at it at that very moment. If someone is smaller or thinner than me I mentally dissect what my strengths and weaknesses would be in that specific instant. If I walk by 2 or 3 or more young "toughs" I instantly size up the situation and see how I would handle the first interaction to most quickly remove myself from the situation. It may seem like a lot of work at first but I promise after a short time it will become second nature; a literal split-second thing. It all boils down to harnessing the power of concentration. Train without ceasing!

Controlled Cruelty and Conditional Apathy

True personal protection grows from internalizing certain concepts, not just techniques: If when performing a drill I say to one of the seminar attendees, "attack the eyes!" They may hesitate for a second at first, as they are waiting for me to tell them *how* to attack the eyes. Once they get the hang of it, the conceptual way of thinking takes over and they are never at a loss for a technique.

Two concepts that are at the forefront of designing your personal self-protection skills toolbox and which must be firmly grasped to succeed at removing yourself from harm are those of *controlled cruelty* and *conditional apathy*.

The concept of controlled cruelty is simply the ability to flip a switch in your head that will allow you to conjure up intense desires to cause the greatest amount of pain and merciless injury to your attacker, employ the techniques in this book in a surgically precise yet ruthless and barbaric way to do just that without remorse or regard for the attacker's safety or well-being, and then just as quickly be able to flip the switch back off once the threat is neutralized. Needless to say, this requires much training and practice to be able to make use of. Part of the training comes from practice of the physical techniques to the point of second nature; another method of training involves being able to make use of everyday situations that cause you to become angry or frustrated and rather than bottling up all of the aggression and rage (which is NEVER a good thing) find a way to recognize how you are feeling, recognize how what you are feeling makes you feel – an idea called a *metaprogram* - and transmute those feelings into the ability to get in touch with that part of you that is capable of barbaric acts of violence. Make no mistake, we all have it in us. I don't give a shit what anyone says-Gandhi or Mother Teresa could have just as easily gouged out someone's eyeball as some convict doing a double life sentence did to his cellmate for not giving him a candy bar. It's all a matter of learning what buttons to push and what each person's switch is.

Conditional apathy is, in its' simplest form, not giving a shit about what the circumstances are you may find yourself in should you need to apply any of these strategies, skills or techniques. This idea, mindset, mentality-whatever you want to call it-is another thing that is easy to pay lip service to but requires dedicated, concentrated effort to harness. The good news is, just like the concept of controlled cruelty, it is something we all have hard-wired into us-it's just a matter of knowing the code, so to speak, and tapping into it.

Conditional apathy is getting to a state of mind where you don't care if you're cut, bleeding, outnumbered or whatever else. A raccoon caught in a corner doesn't care if it's a 98lb. old lady or a 980 lb. grizzly bear who corners it. It lashes out and fights like a whirlwind. This concept is similar to the one of controlled cruelty in that it requires getting in touch with a primal switch embedded deep within your brain and, in fact, the two concepts are symbiotic, meaning that each one thrives off of the other. For example, a meek housewife and mother who would never think of being able to fight off an attacker suddenly jumps on and viciously fends off a mountain lion or coyote that is attacking her child. Had that woman stopped, processed what was going on and *objectively* viewed the situation, I can bet my left pinkie she would have been paralyzed by fear. None of that matters, though- it is her *child* in danger, so all circumstances fly right out the window, and she proceeds to hand that mountain lion a down-home ass whooping, saving her child's life though she sustains severe injuries from its' teeth and claws.

Growing up I was a shark fanatic-hey, what else is a chubby kid going to do after school but head up to the library, right? To this day *Jaws* ranks in my top 5 all-time movie list, and ironically it is through that movie that I became aware of what has come to be a prime example of this principle. My favorite story of conditional apathy is the events surrounding one of the most famous and widely publicized shark attacks in history-that of Australian spearfisherman Rodney Fox. The following description of his ordeal is listed on his website www.rodneyfox.com:

> On the 8th of December 1963, Rodney was defending his title in a spearfishing competition off Aldinga Beach, 65km south of Adelaide, South Australia. The waters were clear and Rodney was just about to catch a fish in about 20m of water when he felt a thump on his left side and found himself in the mouth of a great white shark. Rodney clawed at the sharks head and eyes and, when the shark released its grip, he thrust his right arm out to defend himself only to plunge it into the shark's mouth, slicing the flesh from his hand and forearm. Instinctively, he wrapped his arms and legs around the shark's body to stop it from getting hold of him again but his need for air saw him release and kick for the surface.
>
> *"There, I gratefully gasped one deep breath, then looked down through the water. This was the most terrifying, unforgettable moment of all. My body floated in a red sea and as I looked down through that bloody water, surging upwards through the reddish haze was an open set of jaws with razor-sharp teeth. The shark was coming back to eat me".*
>
> After kicking at the shark, it turned its attention to the fish float, swallowing both the fish and the float, still attached to Rodney's waist. Rodney was dragged back under, spinning uncontrollably as he was dragged deeper and deeper. Just when his breath was

running out, the rope snapped and Rodney kicked for the surface. He was dragged into a nearby boat and carried ashore before being rushed to the nearest hospital.

Rodney's abdomen was fully exposed and all ribs were broken on his left side. His diaphragm was punctured, lung ripped open, scapula was pierced, spleen was uncovered, the main artery from his heart was exposed. The tendons, fingers and thumb in his right hand were all cut, and to this day he still has part of a Great White tooth embedded in his wrist. He was minutes away from his veins collapsing due to the loss of large amounts of blood. Over 360 stitches were required to sew him up.

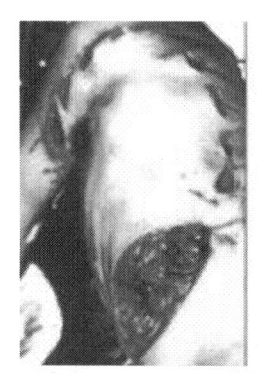

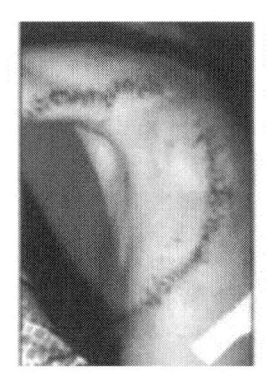

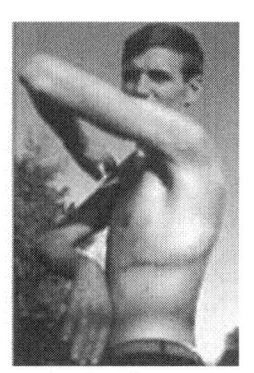

Photos courtesy of Fox Shark Research website www.rodneyfox.com

Stories like this, while terrifying, also serve as a reminder of an immutable Universal Law: the will to survive is always greater than the want to kill. Period.

"Obstacles can't stop you. Problems can't stop you. Most of all other people can't stop you. Only you can stop you."
-Jeffrey Gitomer

FINAL NOTES / PARTING THOUGHTS

Always keep in mind that nothing regarding self-defense is set in stone. You will need to adjust on the drop of a dime so rather than familiarize yourself with "technique-specific" training, learn to familiarize yourself with *target* specific (eyes, throat, groin and secondary target) training and you will never be at a loss for what to do, as there will always be a target at your disposal. It is impossible for someone to physically attack and not simultaneously give you at least one of those targets to work with. This is where training and repetition, repetition, repetition comes in! What would you do if you are caught off guard? Put into a headlock? Ambushed in a hallway or coming out of your car? Sucker punched? How can you train to apply these tools when you are in these situations?

Keep these in mind while you train, and even when you're not training. Always keep your mind alert and your senses sharp, because you just never know.

I'll leave you with my all-time favorite quote regarding all things self-defense and fighting related, this one from Paul Vunak, renowned self-defense pioneer and the former officially contracted & exclusive hand-to-hand close quarter combat instructor to U.S. Navy SEAL Teams:

You will not RISE to your expectations; You will FALL to your level of training.

It has been my sincere pleasure and privilege to write this book for you. Train hard, be smart, stay safe and God bless you and your loved ones. NOW GET TO IT!

BONUS SECTION:

"FIGHTING CHANCE FITNESS"

HOME WORKOUT ROUTINE

Much has been written recently about the importance of the mind/body/spirit connection as it relates to one's overall health and well-being. This idea, however, is nothing new. The ancient Greek and Roman civilizations, for example, personified the phrase *mens sana en corpore sano*, or "a sound mind in a sound body." The samurai of feudal Japan as well as the warrior monks of the Shaolin monastery of China, the birthplace of martial arts, were equally as adept in the ancient warrior arts as they were well versed in the disciplines of philosophy, meditation and Zen. In today's modern society some of these ideas may seem a bit dated however when one really examines the ever-changing, constantly demanding and generally unpredictable world we live in, such emphasis on developing such a connection between our mental, physical and spiritual sides we can see that such a holistic, all-encompassing approach to fitness is really the only way to go to ensure lasting health and happiness.

It comes as no surprise, then, that martial art-based programs offer one a variety of benefits, and there is certainly no shortage of such programs out there. Where the majority of these programs-which do hold many benefits to those who choose to engage in them-fall short, is that they do not adequately address the issue of practicality. The sad fact is (and anyone who even casually glances at the nightly news can vouch for this) is that we live in a world where bad things happen to good people every day. Knowing this, I'd like to be as prepared as possible, wouldn't you? True inner peace stems from knowing that one is able to handle oneself in a variety of situations.

Unfortunately, as stated earlier, this is where many "martial fitness" regimens fall a bit short of their intended goals. Just as one cannot fully appreciate kindness until they have experienced rudeness, those who wish to practice a true "mind/body/spirit" routine cannot achieve that sense of true self-confidence and inner peace until they begin to incorporate a program that addresses martial arts training in such a way that benefits are gained not only from the physical activity that such a program provides but also the knowledge that the moves being practiced can be used in a simple, direct and efficient manner.

This program is based on self-protection strategies employed by various members of America's military and law enforcement communities with some modifications made in order to be easily integrated into your workout cycle. Each of the techniques detailed in this article, when practiced, offer the reader a variety of physical benefits, as well as a way to burn off the stress of a taxing day at work or an argument with a significant other. The techniques utilized in this routine, whose mechanics are demonstrated in detail in the Upper & Lower Body Techniques section of this book, are simple to learn, easy to practice and efficient to use. The greatest benefit of an exercise program is well-being and health. Remember, if you train for HEALTH, the LOOKS will come.

Each of the techniques demonstrated are quite invigorating to practice and very effective should they ever need to be used-talk about a win-win all the way around! Following this plan provides you with endless possibilities while allowing your mind to become fully engaged as well-definitely more fun and energizing than popping on the iPod and enduring your 982nd trip to the elliptical. If you picture yourself in a scenario against a determined attacker, hell bent on killing you or injuring your loved ones, how can exercise possibly be mundane or boring?

TWO QUICK THINGS....

P.S. Here are two products you may find useful in your training:

www.gymboss.com A personal round timer designed to time your active rounds and interval rest sets-it keeps you honest. It's inexpensive and, trust me, it sure beats the hell out of an egg timer.

www.gofit.com Out of all the jump ropes I have used, I prefer the GoFit Speed Rope the best. Its' swivel handle ensures a solid pass each and every time. For 10-12 bucks, why not?

I highly recommend you check out these products-they can help you get the maximum from your time spent working out. Ok, let's get this show on the road. Here goes...

Sample Routine
Warm up-5 minutes (this can be walking/jogging, skipping rope or any blood-pumping exercises followed by light joint rotations such as waist twists, ankle and wrist rotations and arm swings).

Evasion/Parry Footwork- visualize attacks coming in and having to deflect or avoid using body unity and footwork. Repeat for 2 minutes, switching sides every 15 seconds or so.
50 jumping jacks
30 seconds rest

Eyejab- 15 to 20 reps on each side using visualization and shadowboxing, not merely standing in one spot throwing them out there-use visualization and change the tempo, switching stances after each set, i.e., 20 eyejabs with the left hand while keeping your left foot forward, then switch to the right hand with the right foot forward , and so on. Always remember to keep the opposite hand up! Repeat for 2 minutes.
15-20 squats
30 seconds rest

NOTE : Follow the remainder of techniques in this manner-this will ensure both sides get adequate conditioning for all of the techniques listed below

Knee- 12 to 15 reps each leg, repeat for 2 minutes
10-15 pushups
30 seconds rest

Elbow- 15 reps with each arm, repeat for 2 minutes
20-25 crunches
30 seconds rest

Palm strike- 12 reps with each hand, repeat for 2 minutes
12 alternating lunges on each leg (one, one, two, two, etc.)
30 seconds rest

Groin Kick- 12 to 15 reps with each leg, repeat for 2 minutes
10-15 pushups
30 seconds rest

Oblique Kick- 12-15 reps with each leg, repeat for 2 minutes
20-25 crunches
30 seconds rest

Axe Hand (Front/Rear)- 12-15 reps with each hand, repeat for 2 minutes
20-25 squats

Eventually add in two techniques per round, then three, then four and so on until all techniques in this book are available for all of the rounds. Then vary your calisthenics. Eventually you can shorten the rest intervals. There is no limit to variety other than your imagination. Keep the intensity up and your visualization clear and you will be shocked at how quickly you get the heart pumping and the sweat dripping.

Cool down stretching (quads, hamstrings, chest and calves, shoulders, chest and arms)-5 minutes.

Give this routine a whirl, or use the techniques presented above to create your own routine-just be sure to adhere to the circuit training ideas upon which this workout is based. As you become stronger, the dimensions of the sample routine will eventually not challenge you anymore-this is fine. Simply add more reps, blend techniques together (i.e., kick, elbow, knee), increase the number of pushups, squats, etc., in your arsenal and vary the types of pushups, squats, lunges, crunches, etc. The beauty of this program lies in the fact that you can *never* outgrow it! You will get stronger physically but the real kicker (no pun intended) is in the way your mind and body will begin to fuse together while going through this workout; your mind will begin to concoct very persuasive arguments against keeping going when it gets rough but you will not cave.
you will continue;
you will persevere;
and you will win.

"The bottom line is you have no right to expect success if you do nothing to bring it about."
-Matt Furey

"Denial and inactivity prepare people well for the roles of victim and corpse."
— Dr. Leach

APPENDIX A:
820Express Ving Tsun Martial Science Club (820XVT)

In Structure, *Simplicity*
In Technique, *Efficiency*
In Application, *Intensity*
And In All Things, *PRACTICALITY*

The 820Express Ving Tsun Martial Science Club (820XVT) was founded in 2012 by Instructor Robert Bartkowski to promote and preserve the Wong Shun Leung system of Ving Tsun as a combative system of personal protection and sel-empowerment as taught to him by Sifu Philip Ng, himself a direct student of the late Grandmaster and undefeated no-rules challenge fighter Sifu Wong Shun Leung, of the Ng Family Chinese Martial Arts Association, headquartered in Chicago's Chinatown.

For those who may not be aware, Wong Shun Leung was the man directly responsible for instructing a young Bruce Lee in Hong Kong. In fact, Wong Shun Leung's own experience as a street fighter (undefeated in some say hundreds of bare knuckle no-rules challenge matches in Hong Kong) as well as his direct, no-nonsense philosophy of personal protection -having survived several street encounters almost always outnumbered against both unarmed and weapon-toting assailants) inspired Lee in his evolution of his own personal style of martial arts which he termed jeet kune do, *translated as* way of the intercepting fist)

Philip stressed to Robert the need for him to create a more personalized yet standardized vehicle for him to better spread the art of Ving Tsun to his students, thus ensuring the art is passed on in a progressive yet undiluted manner and, in the process, continue to develop and gain deeper understanding of the art himself.

820XVT is dedicated to constant growth and self-learning via the medium of the art and science of Ving Tsun Gung Fu through proper and constant training to attain combat proficiency. It is the belief of 820XVT that true inner peace and self-confidence can only be attained when one inherently understands that he/she can handle him/herself in any enviornment, either by recognizing and avoiding a potentially dangerous situation, verbally diffusing a possible conflict or, if necessary, successfully incapacitating an attacker and removing oneself from harm's way. It is in this spirit that 820XVT was formed.

OUR LOGO
Our logo speaks volumes as to who we are and what type of training we engage in. First, we are a "Martial Science" Club. Why "Martial Science?" Wong Shun Leung called his expression of Ving Tsun, *"Ving Tsun Kuen Hok"* or *"The Science of Ving Tsun."* We do not view Ving Tsun as an "art" per se, although it is. We view Ving Tsun as a scientific, surgically precise yet barbaric when necessary system of personal protection skills and strategies. If other martial art styles and systems can be likened to art classes in high school by way of their aesthetic beauty, Ving Tsun can be compared to physics and geometry, as we are guided by immutable laws and scientific principles.

OUR NAME

Our name *820Express* pretty well sums up what we are all about. Research shows that most if not all real altercations are between 8 and 20 seconds in length, from initial contact-either physical or verbal-to the end of the altercation. This leaves us a very small window to end the conflict on our terms, either by diffusion, verbal de-escalation or should the need arise, physical action. This extremely small window of time necessitates a no-frills, quick and efficient method of physical techniques and strategies. Much the same way as an Express train gets from point A to point B in the quickest amount of time, our philosophy is to avoid physical altercations if at all possible; however, should one need to utilize their skills their only focus should be on terminating the threat. Drills, postures, prearranged sequences and intricate motions get chucked out the window; gross motor skills take over and as such the conflict needs to be resolved NOW. It is for this reason that we hold in our minds' eye the purpose of an Express train when we train…and when we have to use force we want to attack our opponent like they stepped in front of one. Out of these two ideas was born our name, 820Express Ving Tsun.

FIGURES

Of the two figures, you will notice the attacker is larger than the defender. This is because attackers will almost always tend to target those smaller in size, strength, etc., just as a cheetah never picks the fastest or strongest gazelle to hunt. Add this to the fact that the art of Ving Tsun is said to have been founded by a woman and you can see why this art is ideally suited for those who have neither the size nor physical strength to outmatch an attacker by force or physical stature alone.

CHINESE CHARACTERS

The Chinese characters for "Ving Tsun Kuen" pays homage to the traditional nature of the art; i.e., that we train and pass the art on in an undiluted way. Although many members of the club cross-train in different styles, when we train in Ving Tsun it is VING TSUN time. We do not blend or combine the system with others in our classes. This ensures the potency of the art remains intact by a firm grasp and fuller understanding of the concepts and principles of the art.

INTELLIGENCE & INTENSITY
The bottom rocker contains the words "Intelligence" and "Intensity." These are the two adjectives that best describe the spirit in which we train. Ving Tsun is a thinking person's art. We do not do anything that is of no use. Conversely, we must train with intensity so as to be prepared to use our art in a realistic manner should the need ever arise.

CIRCLE
The Circle in the middle of the logo symbolizes constant change and evolution. We are all evolving (or at least should be) as martial artists, fighters and most importantly, as human beings. We chose the modern style of the circle in lieu of the yin/yang symbol to recognize that while our art is more than 350 years old, we live in a fast-paced, constantly changing society and as such, we must adapt to our surroundings and strive to apply our art in today's world without losing the art to bastardization under the guise of "modernization." The fact that the circle is open-ended and not closed pays homage to the notion that we are and never will be perfect; rather we strive to improve a little more each day.

As a hands-on instructor and self-confessed perpetual "white belt," Robert does not coach from the sidelines; he can be found training alongside those in class-bumps, bruises and all. He feels the only way to improve others is to constantly improve oneself. Please feel free to contact us via our website www.makeyourwingchunwork.com

APPENDIX B:
The Wong Shun Leung System
of
Ving Tsun (Wing Chun) Gung-Fu

The Wong Shun Leung system of Ving Tsun (Wing Chun) gung fu is a system of personal protection skills, strategies and techniques based solely on the concepts of simplicity, directness and efficiency. Rather than give the student a technique for every possible scenario, the WSL system makes use of just a handful of basic techniques as well as reflex and sensitivity drills to hone the student's ability to react to an attack with an attack of one's own and without stopping to think of what to do or how to react. In short, if one is not attacking the attacker, one isn't doing WSL Ving Tsun properly! Training is both physically and mentally challenging, as it requires both intelligence and intensity to perform properly. The following synopsis of the WSL method of Ving Tsun was taken from the Ng Family Chinese Martial Arts Association website (www.ngfamilymartialarts.com):

> Ving Tsun is a martial arts based solely upon the principles of simplicity, efficiency and directness. The simpler the actions the easier they are to execute effectively. There are no wasted movements. The only actions taken by the Ving Tsun practitioner during combat are those that are necessary to incapacitate the opponent immediately, nothing more.
> Utilizing direct attacks into their opponent's center while using proper structure and positioning to protect their own, the Ving Tsun practitioner's primary aim is the incapacitation of their opponent. There are no over-elaborate movements within Ving Tsun. Simple movements and simple concepts are all that you will find within the Ving Tsun system.

Ving Tsun contains only three empty hand sequences, one sequence performed on a wooden dummy ("mok jong" as pronounced in Cantonese), and two weapon sets.

Rather than confusing the practitioner with a multitude of situation-specific techniques and sequences, Ving Tsun offers the student concepts and techniques that are adaptive to all combat situations. Many different circumstances can and will arise during actual combat. It is impractical and futile to predict and practice specifically for all the circumstances and situations that might arise. Therefore, Ving Tsun works to familiarize the student not with specifics, but with concepts and principles that are simple, direct, efficient, and adaptive to all levels of combat.

In short, Ving Tsun is a system of simple and adaptive techniques that, when used in conjunction with Ving Tsun's universal principles and concepts, will enable the practitioner with usable tools for self-protection in a violent encounter. In Ving Tsun there is no time wasted on practicing movements that you will never apply. You practice what you use, and you will use what you practice.

The spirit of the Wong Shun Leung (WSL) method of Ving Tsun is nowhere more apparent than in a quote from "the Man" himself, the late Wong Shun Leung:

> "Self-defense is only an illusion, a dark cloak beneath which lurks a razor-sharp dagger waiting to be plunged into the first unwary victim. Whoever declares that any weapon manufactured today, whether it be a nuclear missile or a .38 special, is created for self-defense should look a little more closely at his own image in the mirror. Either he is a liar or is deceiving himself. Wing Chun kung fu is a very sophisticated weapon - nothing else. It is

a science of combat, the intent of which is the total incapacitation of an opponent. It is straightforward, efficient and deadly. If you're looking to learn self-defense, don't study Wing Chun. It would be better for you to master the art of invisibility."
- Wong Shun Leung

Photo courtesy of chisao.com

Grand Master Wong Shun Leung 1931-1997

APPENDIX C: Sifu Philip Ng

Photo courtesy of Philip Ng

Action film star and Ving Tsun (wing chun) instructor of the Author, Sifu Philip Ng immigrated to America from his native Hong Kong at the age of seven. Upon arriving in the United States he began his scholarship of the martial arts with Hung Gar and Choy Lay Fut under the supervision of both his father and uncle. At the age of 13, Philip Ng began his study of Ving Tsun Gung Fu with his uncle Alan Ang and Tae Kwon Do with Master Woon S. Shim. To further his education in the field of Ving Tsun Gung Fu, Philip Ng traveled to Hong Kong and become the student of the great Sifu Wong Shun Leung. He traveled and trained tirelessly with Sifu Wong until his untimely passing early in 1997. Before his untimely passing, Sifu Wong Shun Leung encouraged Philip to begin instructing students in America to become training partners. Thus, Philip Ng initiated the Illini Ving Tsun Association at the University of Illinois at Urbana-Champaign. In addition to being an avid practitioner and instructor of Ving Tsun (Wing Chun) Gung Fu, Philip is also a 6th generation practitioner and instructor of Choy lay Fut Gung Fu under the supervision of his father and teacher, Sifu Sam Ng. Aside from his studies of the Chinese martial arts, Sifu Philip Ng also partakes in the study of arts such as Western Boxing, Korean Tae Kwon Do, Japanese Jujitsu and Filipino Escrima. In his efforts to promote the Chinese martial arts, Sifu Philip Ng has written articles for various national and international martial arts periodicals. In addition to serving as an official for numerous national and international martial arts competitions, Sifu Philip Ng has also coordinated and participated in numerous public performances. Philip currently resides in Hong Kong where he is a working as an actor, action director and martial arts choreographer.

Photos courtesy of Philip Ng

APPENDIX D:
Sifu Joseph Goytia

Photo courtesy of Joseph Goytia

Jeet Kune Do and close quarter combat Instructor to the Author, Sifu Joseph Goytia has been involved in the martial arts for over 30 years. He has several black belts in traditional martial arts such as Tae Kwon Do and Karate. He is a certified instructor in Bruce Lee's Jeet Kune Do and Filipino Kali under two of JKD's top instructors: the late Ted LucayLucay and Paul Vunak, and has extensive training in Brazilian Jiu Jitsu, Indonesian Pentjak Silat and shootwrestling. In combat sports Sifu Goytia has won several championships in boxing and kickboxing during his tour of duty with the US Marine Corps. While in the Marine Corps Sifu Goytia became an instructor of hand-to-hand combat to Marine Corps units. In a civilian capacity he has continued to train Marine Corps personnel in hand-to-hand combat as well as training state and local police. Sifu Goytia is the founder of Intense Defense Systems (www.intensedefensesystems.com) and the founder of the Total Fight Challenge (TFC), the largest licensed MMA event and circuit in the Midwest.

About the Author

Instructor Robert Bartkowski (center) has been studying martial arts since 1994. Robert holds an Instructor's certificate in Wing Chun (Ving Tsun) kung fu from the prestigious Ng Family Chinese Martial Arts Association (NFCMAA) headquartered in Chicago's Chinatown. Robert also holds an Apprentice Instructor certificate in Intense Defense Systems Close-Quarter Combat under Sifu Joseph Goytia, a Phase III Instructor rank in the Proactive Personal Security system of Self-Defense from Empower Training Systems, and a 1st degree black belt/instructor status in taekwondo through the American Taekwondo Association (ATA), the single largest martial arts organization in the world. Robert created the **Walking Weapon Self Protection Skills System** to help educate the general population as to effective, efficient and easily applied self-protection skills, ensuring that decent people everywhere never need to feel helpless again as well as hoping to educate people that one does not need to study martial arts for years and years in order to learn how to protect oneself and one's friends and family.

Testimonials

As much as I can go on as to how valuable this information is, as the saying goes, the "proof is in the pudding." There is no better reference to the effectiveness of a system such as this than the testimonials of those who have taken one of my Workshops and trained with me. From housewives to students, doctors to law enforcement officers, personal recommendations are the highest honor one can bestow and, believe me when I say that I am humbled beyond words for their kind words.

I have found that the techniques taught in class and from the book are easy to learn and can be mastered by any person regardless of size and/or physical ability. Robert is very knowledgeable on the topic and breaks down the techniques to a very basic level for complete understanding. I would HIGHLY recommend this book for anyone who wants to learn simple yet very effective self-defense techniques and strategies. Thank you!
Melissa Wilder

The Walking Weapon System is an invaluable asset to both the experienced martial artist as well as the general public with little or no martial arts experience. There is an emphasis on practical reactions and self-protection skills which can benefit people without much experience and which is often not taught in more traditional martial art schools. These skills do not involve complex multiple step sequences which are usually impossible to remember under the stress of a real attack. These skills are also more universal as opposed to more traditional training of multiple different responses for the same attack in different parts of the body.

The traditional methods may work after multiple years of repetition and practice but will probably not work for the average person. The skills taught here concentrate on more universal gross motor skills which can be applied under stressful conditions. There is also discussion about awareness of surroundings and ways to prevent potential confrontations which is also frequently absent from most traditional training curriculum. I am both a traditional martial artist as well as a professional with very little free time and highly recommend this book for everyone's library. Robert Bartkowski is an extremely knowledgeable instructor and takes the time to correct each person. He teaches each class personally and takes the time to work with each person individually during the class. The Walking Weapon System classes are high energy classes teaching simple and efficient trapping, striking, and kicking techniques in a reality based scenario. They take into account real-life situations and teach direct and efficient responses. Situational sparring and testing your techniques are emphasized so that you can evaluate and improve your training. Robert's philosophy is to share all knowledge with the students to improve their techniques. I would highly recommend this system and any of Robert Bartkowski's classes or products to anyone.
Robert June, MD (Emergency Room Physician)

Bob,

Fantastic! You will be glad to know that this stuff is EXACTLY what I was taught in the academy. The concept of jamming the attack and closing the space on someone throwing a haymaker was very familiar. The ready stance is also exactly the same, if our instructor caught us on the mat with our hands down, or in a fist, he would slap us one in the chest. We also spent a lot of

time learning how to fall down, recover, keep our legs towards the attack and protect our heads... practicing falling down sucks, especially for big guys. The bigger they are the harder they fall. Man, was I sore! See you on Monday.
Kevin Keenan, Correctional Officer

On behalf of the Lovely and Noble Sisters of Gamma Phi Omega from Loyola University Chicago, I would like to say Thank- You to Bobby for teaching terrific, simple, useful, realistic, effective and very much needed self defense tactics to the college students. Bobby was fun, engaging and informative. He kept the crowd interested with his clever mixture of humor and sincerity.
Everyone in the crowd had a chance to practice their new self defense techniques on the very well padded and protected "perpetrator" Bobby. He was very supportive, encouraging and tolerant of our "attacks." Great Job Bobby, we learned a lot!
Marlisa Quetell
Gamma Phi Omega Sorority
Loyola University Chicago

Hi Bob,

I want you to know that I like your book a lot. It is very well written and easy to understand. Being a law enforcement officer, Self-Defense is major part of my everyday job, being ready for any type of situation, physical or otherwise. The points you make about the non-aggressive stance are right on, you can react to any aggressor from this stance-it's a stance I'm in on a daily basis being on calls. My wife also read your book, she surely enjoyed it. For someone who has never had any self-defense instruction, she picked it up very quickly. It also changed her mindset on how much self-defense is a

really important aspect of life, because you just never know!!!!
Michael Lynch Jr., Police Officer

I have been a police officer for thirteen years and the concepts in Bob's book really work! I have used quite a number of these techniques and concepts on the streets. These concepts have certainly helped me come home unharmed to my family at the end of the day. These concepts and techniques are the foundation for my own personal self defense. If you only read one book on self defense make sure it is this one. This book could help save your life one day!
James Holt, Police Officer

I am a 31 year old teacher, licensed realtor and mother. For the first five years of my career I worked in the Englewood area of Chicago. Our parking lot was in an alley, and I would come and go when it was dark. Needless to say safety was a concern of mine. To be honest, though, I have always been concerned about my safety regardless of where I was at. Being a petite woman I feel like I am a target for any lurking predator. I felt the need to learn how to defend myself, so I decided to attend Bob's self defense class designed for women. Walking into the class I felt weak and helpless. However, as the class progressed, I became more empowered. Bob did not fill our heads with misconceptions nor show us fancy, unrealistic flips that we would probably forget how to do in a time of panic. The message was to be practical, fierce, and mean! Bob taught us the idea is to GET AWAY in the event of an attack, not to restrain your attacker. Therefore, us women must do anything possible like claw with our nails, kick the shins, or, of course, go for the groin! Once you break free, just run away. I highly recommend any woman, mother, sister,

or friend attend one of Bob's self-defense classes or read and really practice the techniques and concepts contained in his book!
Mary Ellen Derman
Schoolteacher & Licensed Realtor

The Walking Weapon Self Protection Skills System is simple in its' technique base, practical in its' application and the techniques are effective for people of all ages and are not dependent on size or strength. I can speak from a uniquely qualified vantage point, having been a soldier in the elite 82nd Airborne Division as well as suffering an injury in the line of duty which necessitated my medical retirement from the U.S. Army. The soldier in me appreciates the no-B.S, get in and get-out nature of the System, while having to deal with certain medical limitations makes me appreciate the System's non-focus on attributes such as size or physical strength to incapacitate an assailant. Always remember that every one of us have limitations; injuries, lack of size or strength, age, and so on but limitations are not limits. There are no limits - if you refuse to limit yourself.
SPC John Fagan
U.S. Army (Ret)
82nd Airborne Division
Graduate of United States Army Ranger School

The following is a very touching testimonial written by the mother of a young man with Down's syndrome who took our course in order to gain basic self-defense skills and improve cognitive motor function. It was an absolute pleasure to teach this young man and seeing him improve himself was more rewarding than can be put into words...

Dear Bob,

It is with great pleasure that I write this letter. I wish to thank you for teaching my son Russ in your Walking Weapon Self Protection Skills class. My son has Down's syndrome. He is 18 years old. This class was perfect for teaching Russ how to protect himself. Thank you for arranging a private class. Russ can process information easier if there is less noise and commotion. The class was for Russ only but I came along to learn so that I could help Russ practice all the moves at home.

Thank you for your easy to understand instructions. Thank you for taking the time to demonstrate each move and then let Russ repeat the move. You gave Russ time to repeat each step over and over. He learns best this way! You talked to Russ and made him pretend to be in a place of danger. You told him to imagine himself walking down the street, entering his home, shopping at the store, etc. You played the "attacker" and let Russ respond. Russ is a visual learner and this "play acting" helped him. You put special leg, arm, face and chest pads on and let Russ practice all the moves-right on you! This was so realistic and helped Russ understand. You gave him an easy to read list of self defense moves. Russ was able to read this list and use it to practice. I recommend your class to anyone & any age. Parents of children with special needs should definitely consider your class. I am planning on having Russ take periodic refresher classes from you. Thank you! You are an excellent Self-Defense Instructor.
Sincerely,
Janet Rickert (Russ' mom)

No, Janet – thank you…and thank *you* for taking the time to read this section of the book; it is without hesitation or exaggeration the single most important one in the entire book to me. Please let me know how the information presented in this Course serves you. I am always here to help you in any way I can. Together we can make this world a safer, better place. We all have to share this big spinning rock; therefore, it is each of our responsibility to make it better for all of us.

May good fortune and health for you and your families never cease and may the need for any of what is discussed in this book never arise.

Thank you once again, and may God Bless you all.

SOME THINGS TO KEEP IN MIND...

Be prepared. - Boy Scout Motto

It wasn't raining when Noah built the ark. - Howard Ruff

Preparation through education is less costly than learning through tragedy. - Max Mayfield, Director National Hurricane Center

Remember; when disaster strikes, the time to prepare has passed. - Steven Cyros

You are responsible for what happens to you. - Fr. Frog

You won't have trouble if you are prepared for it. - Fr. Frog

There's no harm in hoping for the best as long as you're prepared for the worst. - Stephen King

Speak softly and carry a big stick; you will go far. - Theodore Roosevelt

Don't hit at all if it is honorably possible to avoid hitting; but never hit soft!
 - Theodore Roosevelt

It usually takes me two or three days to prepare an impromptu speech. - Mark Twain

Over the years, Americans in particular have been all too willing to squander their hard-earned independence and freedom for the illusion of feeling safe under someone else's authority. The concept of self-sufficiency has been undermined in value over a scant few generations. The vast majority of the population seems to look down their noses upon self-reliance as some quaint dusty relic, entertained only by the hyperparanoid or those hopelessly incapable of fitting into mainstream society.
- Cody Lundin

Chance favours the prepared mind. - Louis Pasteur

Connie drove a silver Camry with rosary beads hanging from her rearview mirror and a Smith & Wesson stuck under the seat. No matter what went down, Connie was covered.
- Janet Evanovich

Prepare for the unknown by studying how others in the past have coped with the unforeseeable and the unpredictable.
- Gen. George S. Patton

We are not preparing for the world we live in - we are preparing for the world we find ourselves in. - Michael Mabee

Don't rush in order to have things done early. Be prepared before you set off. That's the rule. However, this does not mean that you keep delaying the time for beginning. You must begin by all means! Go, get prepared! - Israelmore Ayivor

Preparation doesn't assure victory, it assures confidence. - Amit Kalantri

Your responsibility to be ready for the fight never ends. - James Yeager

By failing to prepare, you are preparing to fail. - Benjamin Franklin

Another way to be prepared is to think negatively. Yes, I'm a great optimist but, when trying to make a decision, I often think of the worst case scenario. I call it 'the eaten by wolves factor.' If I do something, what's the most terrible thing that could happen? Would I be eaten by wolves? One thing that makes it possible to be an optimist, is if you have a contingency plan for when all hell breaks loose. There are a lot of things I don't worry about, because I have a plan in place if they do.
- Randy Pausch

What has mood to do with it? You fight when the necessity arises—no matter the mood! Mood's a thing for cattle or making love or playing the baliset. It's not for fighting.
- Frank Herbert

An ounce of prevention is worth a pound of cure. - Benjamin Franklin

If you believe you can accomplish everything by "cramming" at the eleventh hour, by all means, don't lift a finger now. But you may think twice about beginning to build your ark once it has already started raining. - Max Brooks

There is always a part of my mind that is preparing for the worst, and another part of my mind that believes if I prepare enough for it, the worst won't happen. - Kay Redfield Jamison

*The will to win is nothing without the will to prepare.
- Juma Ikangaa*

*It's best to have your tools with you. If you don't, you're apt to find something you didn't expect and get discouraged.
- Stephen King*

Opportunity is a haughty goddess who wastes no time with those who are unprepared. - George S. Clason

Good luck is a residue of preparation. - Jack Youngblood

*We have to prepare for the worst, and the worst is war.
- Bernard Kouchner*

*To perform you need practice, to practice you need passion.
- Amit Kalantri*

Dedication

This book is dedicated to my aunt, Sharon Hamrick, who fought her battle with Amyotrophic Lateral Sclerosis (ALS), or Lou Gehrig's Disease, like a true champion. Though she was a physically small, gentle and unimposing woman she had the heart of a lion.

My aunt Sharon (seen to the left in the above photograph) walking across the finish line at the 2003 Chicago Les Turner ALS Foundation Walk for a Cure. She told my mother that, while she may have been pushed in a wheelchair, she would finish by walking across that line on her own two feet-and so she did.

Your courage will *always* inspire me and give me strength.

*Author Robert Bartkowski
is available for
workshops/seminars, speaking engagements,
private & group training and
Instructor Certification Courses.*

Pricing & scheduling inquiries may be sent to:

bobby@selfprotectionskills.com

Bob discussing his views on self-defense and personal protection.

Manufactured by Amazon.ca
Bolton, ON